Organic Matter

E.N. Couturier

Autofocus Books
Easton, Pennsylvania

Published by Autofocus Books
autofocusbooks.com

Edited by Lena Crown

Memoir/Literature
ISBN: 978-1-957392-38-7
Library of Congress Control Number: 2025931959

Cover design by Amy Wheaton
Cover image: "Windsor Style Tablet-Arm Chair from Monticello" from the Digital Public Library of America, via its partner Heartland Hub, uploaded to Wikimedia Commons by the Missouri Historical Society, rendered to illustration by Amy Wheaton

Organic
Matter

For everyone taking a chance or trying to figure it out, with deep thanks to my mother and dad, all farms that hire young people, and everyone else along the way, however things may have turned out in the end.

My knees hurt from the inside out and are difficult to bend. When I squat, they crack like cap guns; when I straighten them, they make the sharp snapping sound of popcorn in a microwave. Nobody can tell me why. Sitting through my college classes, I catch myself in the posture of someone writing a bad check on a department store counter.

In two months, I start work on a vegetable farm, but I still haven't learned how to suffer. I've spent the past six summers laboring on trails or in landscaping or at conservation centers, afflicted by every second and going back for more. I started because I wanted to save the environment and hacking at invasive plants with a saw was all that I could understand. Then I found I could barely tolerate the discomfort, and came to see this as a serious character flaw that touched everything in my life but could be fixed with enough effort and must be to make any good use of my time on earth.

For some reason I believe farm work will have a clear enough purpose that I can learn to love it and be made better by it. A tumbleweed of guilt bounces along behind me about this, about going back to the farm with such precious ideas after how hard my parents and grandparents worked to allow me to choose differently. At a certain point, though, you have to just do something and quit agonizing over it (that's what the part of me who is tired of my ineffectual urbanity says).

It's hard to admit I believe in anything so earnestly, that I buy into the idea of the earth changing us, but I do.

As graduation approaches, I'm at the end of a hallway in my life and am finding no doors there, just one thick window. I can punch through the glass with my knuckles and jump and land bleeding on the dirt outside if I want to live badly enough to risk it, which sometimes I am tempted to doubt.

I didn't understand what I would use a college degree for, but it seemed bad things would happen if I didn't go, and I was lucky to be able to, and what else was there? Now I am supposed to apply to graduate school. But I'm terrified of debt, which I avoided in undergrad by going to a tiny local college, and I don't want to sit alone in a room for eight years, and once I got that degree, what good would it help me do? Wouldn't more school just delay that question?

When I finally decided to farm, that was how I explained it: I'm not crazy, I'm not dropping out of society, I'm just learning new things about the world, I'm perfectly calm, and all of this is normal.

On my first day of work, I woke up from a good dream with blood in my nose.

The night before, I sat on my stoop alone eating microwaved soup from a box. Society!

The forty-minute drive from the city to the farm, through the suburbs and out flat onto the earth, felt like undergoing something surgical. I kept switching radio stations, thinking about what the person I wanted to be when I arrived would listen to. My station wagon is the same age as I am, and I worry about how it will handle all this distance. Maybe we'll all like each other and decide to carpool.

It took months to find this job. Other people want to change their lives too—who knew? As rejections came in, I feared I had given the wrong answer to what I would be if I were a vegetable (only freaks are eggplants!!!) or had some kind of overeducated, underexperienced squishiness about me that everyone else could see.

The email from my future boss starting with *Hey, congrats!* arrived in my Monday morning research methods class during a presentation on how to design an appealing thesis poster. My final semester had been dedicated to researching the loss of productive farmland in Michigan over the past fifty years, reading about people who probably understood labor very well, or were never distant enough from it to think about it this much in the first place.

Four days on, two days off, the email said, plus working the market downtown on Saturdays. Serif fonts alienate and disturb your audience by disrupting the visual field, as do gradient backgrounds. Five acres of vegetables, also a couple rows of popcorn and some chickens behind the house, but you don't have to worry about those, I take care of them on my own time.

I told my professor about the job on my way out of the classroom and he said, Oh, well, look at you. I called my parents and they said, Oh, okay, that's great. I walked to the library to work on my thesis and felt so happy I could have ripped through the 1970 census books in my arms with my teeth, just to get the intensity of the feeling out of me.

My coworkers started last week while I walked across the graduation stage and went out to brunch. When I showed up this morning, they were darting around the farmyard carrying black plastic trays of lettuce seedlings without looking up. Boss came out of the main wash barn and introduced me around. He's a good-natured guy twice my age whom I like a lot, but he has this kind of distance from the rest of us, in his mannerisms but also literally—I only saw him in the morning.

Kristy, who has the responsibilities of a farm manager but the same title as the rest of us, is in her fifth season. She directed everything we did and told me right away to sign up for food stamps, which all the farm's employees qualify for. This job is not going to provide for you, so don't think it will, she said while we picked blades of grass from bins of cut salad greens.

Pena, a small and sensible-seeming person, is still in college and worked for years at a student farm. He wears a scapular that flaps around and gets caught on things and sticks to the sweat on his neck. Gwynn looks like a teenager but is actually thirty. She lives an hour and a half away and spent the past decade working in a kitchen supply store.

They all remind me of people I've met before; to me they are the same people, and we already know each other from the student newspaper and the grocery store and that friend of a friend's weird boyfriend who was a competitive pogo stick bouncer.

Harvested rainbow radishes from the hoop house while it rained. You have to squeeze their girth to make sure they don't feel woody, which indicates they are too old. Most of them were no good anyway. They split in half at their pointed bottom due to too much water. It's amazing how many obvious things I do not know and signs I never learned to see.

The best way to rubber-band bunches is to arrange five radishes upside down like a star in the curve between your thumb and index finger. Then you loop the band around one radish where it starts to sprout its green, circle around the whole bunch, and secure the rubber band over one neighbor past where you started.

Gwynn was so frustrated by the process that she almost started to cry. We weren't talking at all before that, just pulling radishes from the mud in windy silence. She wears enormous men's construction boots with skinny jeans and looks tethered to the ground when she walks.

My boyfriend donated my boots to the Goodwill by accident, she said, And most of my clothes.

I know a lot about Gwynn's personal life already. She seems like the type of person who can sense every single thing wrong with the world but has no idea what to do next.

Pena, who is studying greenhouse management at State and stands barely five feet tall, looked over at her once without pretending to look away. He has an eerie kind of gaze—very knowing. He asked if I was Catholic too since I went to a college named after a saint. I don't understand or relate to other religious people besides my parents, and bringing myself to church every week causes me chest pains. I said yes, but wanted to warn him that I probably wasn't in the way he thought, wanted to prove the same thing to the other two, under a wave of uncertainty already.

Try to keep pace with us, Kristy leaned over to say to Gwynn, and I had to look down at the ground then in case being part of the situation was about to feel too painful. It seems early in the game for people to be crying, but I want to have a positive outlook.

I *am* trying, Gwynn said.

She has this little boy's haircut that she can't keep out of her eyes. My throat burned looking at all of it, and I tried to enjoy arranging those little radish stars in my hand and enjoy the fact that I was able to do it, too, as if I hadn't just learned how.

Kristy didn't say anything else after that. I turned my eyes heavenward like a statue in church during this exchange, asking for deliverance, which I've got to stop doing because it looks so obviously martyred. Funny how I think I can escape the moments of life I find uncomfortable, and how I experience the shame in every one of those moments even if it isn't my own.

The radishes took four hours. I don't know the last time I repeated one task for that long. We had extra time at the end of the day and flung dirt clods out of the field where the onions will go next week. Shoulders popping from the momentum. Scrambling around in the dust like a photograph in a textbook.

Sort of tense for a first day, really, but on the drive home I felt pretty good without having any idea what about, and had to work hard at keeping my hands on the wheel, at not just flying away along the road.

Saw my friends Shane and Tiny tonight like usual. We walked to the bar for a pitcher and afterwards heated up a few cans of five-bean chili which we ate on their porch, and by then I was so tired my eyelids felt hot.

Transplanted nine rows of onions in the sun; we need to work with both hands moving in different directions. The onions are just tiny tubes of green sticking up four inches from blocks of soft dark soil that fall apart once we shake them from their trays. Kristy and I drew the rows and the plant spacing within them by dragging the dibbler, a rolling cage punctuated with carefully placed spikes, in a straight line behind us. To get the lines straight you have to hold the dibbler handles at the same height and walk at the same speed as the other person.

I try to detach myself from the physical to make it all easier, but I think I am just too bound to everything, and all of it back to me. In the blood and in the ground.

The schedule: Monday and Tuesday morning we harvest for the midweek CSA share, which people subscribe to and pick up pre-portioned. This model is supposed to help the boss pay his bills in the spring. Through Thursday we plant and prune and mow and till and weed, and Friday we harvest again for the market. Each crop is picked into a particular container that fits a particular amount, for easy record-keeping and packing. The big green bins hold sixteen heads of lettuce and the yellow trays fit twelve bags of microgreens.

In the evenings my knees won't bend and the caps feel full of fluid. They're wide to look at and solid to touch. When I get home, I lie down and put my feet up against the wall, trying to drain everything back to where it came from.

I live on the bottom floor of a subdivided house in a neighborhood built for workers at factories that closed decades ago. My roommate, Sarah, who I found on Facebook after the last one moved out to get married, boils eggs every evening to eat before she logs onto her remote finance job the next day. The sulfur comes in under my door. She pays rent annoyingly early. We don't like each other; our cheap old apartment is in bad shape.

Logically, it's clear that I don't need to live this way, but at the same time, I have to, somehow. In every situation, I feel like I'm just not quite right, no matter how hard I try and try again. I think too much and ask too many questions. God is trying to talk to me, and I can't hear. My questions are less about belief and more about what to do next.

Growing up, my family's problems were worse than most, but not so extreme that I feel justified in being this troubled. My mother used to be crazy and then had a vision of Jesus, who told her to go back to church. We did this, and in time she became less crazy. Even having witnessed a miracle, I'm still adrift and confused. If that's not enough for me, what will be?

My life was given to me for some reason, and I'm not sure I'm qualified to figure out what it is.

I also live with a squirrel who has made a home in my bedroom wall and keeps me up at night scrabbling around. When I call our landlord about this, he says he's working on it. I play YouTube videos of sonic screams designed to frighten rodents away. It doesn't work, but I wonder if it's warping me psychologically, since I'm an animal too.

When I bring my legs down from the wall, they feel the same. It's already hard to get to the ground but somehow every morning I'm able to do it again. This gives me hope that I'm doing what I am supposed to.

So far, I have been most surprised by the difficulty of thinking one step to the next. Boss will write "carrot harvest" on the whiteboard and disappear and leave us to figure out the rest. He's busy grinding the lead paint off the walls of the white farmhouse, which looks abandoned though he's lived in it for ten years. So many small things have to be done to complete one larger task, and every one of them could be executed wrong or inefficiently in about a hundred ways.

I can feel my brain stretching to accommodate these new considerations, making me sweaty and strange and scared until it clicks, the way I used to feel approaching a new kind of math problem. It also reminds me of my first season working outside, when throughout the summer the urgency and weight and danger of everything boiled a lot of nonsense out of me. Tiny liked to joke that I turned into a country girl as a result of that landscaping job, quiet and impatient, but she couldn't say that about me here; everybody talks all day.

Just this week I learned that Gwynn and her boyfriend have a ferret recently diagnosed with cancer and are both struggling with alcoholism, that Kristy's father is a golf pro who is disappointed in her failure to become a business executive, and that Pena's parents pushed his siblings out of the house at eighteen but want him, the youngest, to stay forever. His father recently made him a new rocking chair to sit in beside his mother while watching television, since Pena had outgrown his old one from the first grade.

I don't know what to say about myself. My dimensions have already disappeared because I am so tired and focused on the immediate. All these ideas about my inner life are coming up short, which I knew they would, and which I wanted to be wise enough not to worry about. I almost told Gwynn that I think about God pretty much every second of the day but never get any further, that I'm circling some fortress I can't enter but leading myself in the wrong direction at the same time, and then I imagined her telling me I sound like I have obsessive compulsive disorder. She's already diagnosed Pena with autism.

That first Friday night, I talked to my friend Red on the phone while I made dinner. We met two summers ago working on the trails at a nature center and he lives out West now. Because we see the world the same way, I end up convinced I should love him even though neither one of us wants that. When he heard the rustling as I emptied a paper bag of salad greens into a bowl, he asked me was I releasing a flock of doves, or something.

I worked my first farmers market and now I understand how gorillas feel sitting behind their special glass walls at the zoo. We're on the other side and every person in the world goes screaming by. If they stop to look, they don't mean anything by it.

Market is down the street from my apartment, which will be convenient on odd-numbered weekends. Every other weekend, I will drive out to the farm before daybreak, load up the van, drive it back here, work until the afternoon, drive it back to the farm, and drive myself home. Gwynn did that today.

It's still freezing in the mornings, and the roof over the market transforms it into a wind tunnel, a long concrete tube with open sides following the downhill slope of the parking lot. Permanent wood tables are built in between the roof support beams. This is nice but means there's no way to get from our side into the market itself without walking ten minutes to its very start or very end. It's so packed with people that I turn aggressive, imagining fighting through them with my elbows, gnashing my gorilla teeth.

Our neighboring vendor, Ryan, sells painted pinecones and little people made out of acorns and pipe cleaners. As we were setting up, he cut his hand on his hunting knife peeling an apple and sprayed blood all over the concrete. He said it looked like a constellation. He's got five little dots tattooed by the side of his right eye and the ink bleeds out into the folds of his skin. Ryan's mother makes the acorn folk and he sells them because she doesn't like real people.

The two of us named the bloody stars. He tried to wash them away with water from the old glass cranberry juice bottle he drinks from, but the blood stayed. I was thinking, *Is this what I'm waiting for?* and wishing I could push my brain through a sieve to stop myself from being so stupid.

Gwynn stood behind us laughing. When she's in the mood to laugh she does it constantly, sounding like she's on the business end of a gun. Kristy walked by carrying a bag full of fancy cooking mushrooms and pretended not to know us.

Hot by noon. Ryan talks so confidently to everyone that I feel almost afraid of him.

Today, Monday, we listened to music in the barn and scrubbed dirty rotting lettuce from the harvest bins all morning while it rained. Tomorrow we'll cut more salad mix into them with our small knives. Against the cold concrete, my legs felt stiff and disconnected from the rest of me.

The wash-and-pack barn was built last summer and has long drains in its middle where we squeegee all the vegetable waste from packing, the weeds and the insect-chewed leaves. Everything rots there until Boss scrapes it out with a big metal shovel. While we scrubbed, he banged on the rickety red tractor parked outside the low-slung older barn that stores tools and garbage. All of the farm equipment is old; modern commercial farms are so large that the things made for them wouldn't fit in our small rows. He forgot to put the plastic bucket over the Farmall's front pipe yesterday and it filled up with water.

One time, he said, a bird got stuck in there and fried alive while he was sowing buckwheat cover crop into a field. Nothing he could do; it was already trapped, and the metal was hot.

I'm surprised by how disgusting the growing process is, but I am becoming part of it already, touching my eyes with fertilizer on my hands and eating around the worms in my lettuce.

Kristy brought in a big bag of moose jerky and shared it with us at lunch. We eat around a picnic table under the maple tree in front of the new barn. The table is waterlogged and splintering, so we sit in rusting metal chairs with the picnic seats as footrests. Kristy's dad paid a lot of money for the moose hunting trip with some business buddies a few years ago.

That's all I know about her, other than that her sister converted to Mormonism to get married and the temple wedding scared Kristy so much she cried through the whole thing. After she told me this, while we packaged overgrown pea shoots in plastic bags for market, she looked at me like I'd made her say it. I mean, I get why people believe in God, but that was different, she said, sniffing and readjusting her sun-bleached baseball hat.

She doesn't know what I believe— that God is real, sees us all, and has a higher use for our lives that is inaccessible to me personally due to the fact that I am weak, undisciplined, and poor of spirit in ways I am failing to cure—because I don't talk about it. I see the holes in this reasoning, and don't apply it to anyone else, but looking at the streetlights through my window blinds at night and trying to feel something from prayer, I can't get past it.

If I said any of this aloud, I fear my coworkers would think I believed the same things about them. It doesn't make sense that I don't. When we sit around the table I just think, *There you are!* Then again, struggling is evidence that I am like everybody else. Maybe sharing it would imply that I don't see myself as above them. When I tried to talk to my college friends about God, they teased me for being self-serious. It seems shameful to strive to be different than you are, like you're condemning others by changing yourself. Such is Midwestern psychology.

I kept quiet, imagining that my talking caused harm in the name of God like all the people before me (oh yeah? Was Jesus afraid to be seen? Isn't it selfish to worry this much?). Whatever you do, whoever you are, you'll lose somehow.

The moose tasted like beef. Gwynn wouldn't eat it; she's a vegetarian, and orders all her food from an online meal preparation subscription service. We get free "seconds" produce, the vegetables left after market or not good enough to send there, but she doesn't take it because her needs are already portioned out.

We've been harvesting spinach by snapping each leaf with our fingernails, and salad greens by holding big chunks and sawing them with small knives—not too close to the base, so that they will regrow in a week or two. Grass grows in between the plants and gets harvested too. We have to pick all the blades out in the barn without losing time. Pick them out, stuff the greens into bags, and make sure the bags all weigh exactly three-quarters of a pound. You have to leave air inside when you tie off so that the leaves don't rot too fast from having something pressed against them.

Boss told me, while we dug around in the old barn for tools to repair the hoop house ventilation fans, that he retains his romanticism about growing things. I was trying very hard to remember where he took each item from so I could replace it in the exact location later.

His shuffling gait became more visible on the flat dirt floor. He shattered his ankle skateboarding a few years ago and hasn't walked the same since. Now that I know it, I can see this in him, somebody who approaches the world as something to have fun jumping and twisting around on, with this kind of cheerful blindness to the dark possibilities of anything.

I hoped that I would develop a romanticism here, but I haven't yet. I don't want the necessary activities of life, like growing and building and laboring, to be a pressure that my humanity can't withstand. In a way, I suppose I just keep pushing on the bruise expecting it to stop hurting. Trying to break through to something, anything.

Last month I read a book for school explaining that medieval serfs lived in a world without time, tethered only to the land and to their hands. I don't find this to be true at all. The earth appears here like a profit surface that we move inputs around on. That book said the world was also a continuous, undifferentiated spiritual experience for the serf, not yet segmented into thought and reason and a small compartment for God, like it is for us. It was news to me that my experience is supposed to be separate like that. I have the same fields as everyone who came before, the same brain to think about it all with.

Later, I was up on a ladder holding the big square metal vent in place above my head while Boss secured it to the hoop house frame with the whining drill, sending thin curlicues of metal fluttering down to the grass. He asked me if I was an apologetic person. I think he said it because I had said I was sorry for being scared to climb up so high.

Well, I guess so, I said, But I'm trying not to be.

It was an embarrassing question to answer, but it would have been more embarrassing not to. I asked him, What about you?

Not one bit! he said, turning the last screaming screw into the metal.

Red hasn't answered my last message about talking on the phone again. Whenever we get close, he disappears for a few months; I barely feel much about it, only run through those channels in my mind because they're already there, which makes me sad and disappointed with myself.

Then I enforce time limits before writing back when I do hear from him again, even though retribution goes against my principles. Most of the time sticking to the principles is enough to protect you, even if you're a mess and can't understand anything that happens. As the time goes on, though, it's harder and harder to see how the principles apply.

That's when I'm tempted to cut and run, take the coward's way out.

I think a lot about going back East, where the rest of my family is from. My parents moved around every few years for most of my life, looking for somewhere that felt better. I want to know how to stay, even when it's difficult. I want to be strong enough to live in a way that God doesn't need to appear in a vision to correct. It's hard to accept that life might always be this difficult, and instead I suppose I need to think the fault lies in me and is therefore fixable. That's partly why everything seems so serious right now—if I can't make it here, can I make it somewhere else, or is it just impossible when you're in the wrong place?

In the morning, a bird flew under the black plastic netting that covers the lettuce heads, which is meant to keep birds away from them. We stood and looked at it thrashing.

Somebody go down there and hold the other end while I lift this one, Kristy said. Gwynn was already crawling under the netting, flinging it away to her right side, and Kristy yelled at her not to step on the produce, but three heads were already crunched under those big boots. Twelve dollars gone.

Pena stood behind us, staring straight-faced with those big eyes. I think we are all somewhat afraid of how little wasted feeling he has in him—of any kind, even social, even graceful.

The bird flew off, out the end of the tunnel and across the soybean field separating our farm from the state highway.

The ends of the netting are sharp and scratch us whenever we unroll it, and Gwynn's arms looked raw for the rest of the day. Her shirt had little plastic pearls sewn onto it spelling out the word BABY; she can't afford to buy work clothes. We make ten dollars an hour and she drives three hours round-trip to get here every day in a car from 1989 because her boyfriend prefers classics.

She kept telling us how it hurt when her sweat rolled down into her open skin, and how it hurt in a different way later, when we were sanitizing the plastic display trays for market. We use hoses that pull down from the barn ceiling and big pump pressure sprayers of diluted hydrogen peroxide.

You know, hydrogen peroxide actually *eats* your flesh, she yelled over her scrub brush while we scraped old, wet lettuce from the plastic bins in the afternoon. When the lettuce is pressed against the plastic it seems to weld to it. We take turns choosing music to play over the speakers in the wash barn; Gwynn was blasting a whispery song about collecting bugs. When I went to put something on for the seventh round of bins, her account was still pulled up. We had been listening to a playlist she named "for having sex to."

I'm never any less fascinated by other people's relationships, and all of my own still surprise me. I mean, just the very fact that any of this exists.

Red called again on Wednesday night. My friend, Red. We were on the line for almost six hours and I could hear the night bugs and the passing trains on the other end. It's warmer out there in Montana, where he now lives and researches trout, and earlier.

He likes to say that there is a lot to love about Montana, as if that's something no one would believe. I've lived so many places that I could probably love anywhere. If you don't think you could love a place eventually, you can't survive it.

Red doesn't seem to understand what I'm doing and I don't know how to explain myself, or feel the desire to anymore; I keep thinking, falsely, that I finally have a life composed of actions that speak for themselves.

I wish he would just keep talking, and I could just hold the phone to my ear until he said goodbye.

He, too, is deeply concerned that I am not in graduate school. It frustrates me to hear that I am wasting my brain and therefore my life if I am not applying it to research papers about people more alive than me whose realities I haven't even come close to understanding. I had in my head somehow that he would always know what I meant without my having to say it, although I possess no evidence to justify this, other than the one time he said the same thing to me.

Told him how I like the experience of working on something that is endless yet provides (proverbial) fruits every day. He compared this to his experiences at the seminars and started talking about linguistics. Learning how to speak refines the soul, he said.

I have been thinking, and failed to explain, that farming is not designed *in service of us* on the personal level, for the development of our character or outputs beyond the survival of ourselves and others (eating spinach, getting tan), and any benefit to the soul appears secondary. The more I see things eaten, rotting, growing unharvested and going to seed, the more I think there's no such thing as a unity with nature or anything physical, just a struggle to control it.

The ground doesn't care what I learn, who I am. I'm serving it rather than the other way around. Maybe that's what he worries about.

All this, on the phone, didn't speak for itself. I just sat there on the porch watching cars rattle by, trying to piece together what to say next to keep him talking, to get him to continue having things to say to me. He has this thoughtful and unshakeable voice, like he knows how to consider the whole world. I want to write down everything he says or maybe record it so I can hold it to my ear all day.

I guess he's probably just lonely out there, but I don't mind if that's the only reason he's talking to me so much, because then I can see him as a real person with faults rather than a figure at a perfect distance. Sitting there with my legs falling asleep on the pebbled concrete of my stoop, feeling my arms on either side of me, I had this sudden experience of my body as a building, something solid and not alive at all.

Our hands are bound by the confines of our language, he told me, and I said, Mm-hm.

Feeling resentful of the energy my body expends to tell me it is unhappy.

Stringing twine between T-posts to hold tiny pea vines off the ground, whose beds are covered in straw that makes me sneeze well into the night.

Watching grandfathers and sons fish over the bridge in the afternoon.

Weeding and weeding and weeding.

Feeling very soft and permeable, emotionally speaking, in the evenings.

Having very personal conversations with Gwynn that I want to escape while they're happening, and incredibly surface-level chats with Kristy that make me equally uncomfortable in another way. Listening to Pena tell me about his pest management courses.

Harvesting for market on Fridays, crossing it all off the whiteboard list and packing crates into the cooler room.

Being tailgated aggressively by a school bus which then flies past me, almost eviscerating an oncoming tractor in the other lane. Imagining the schoolchildren cheering and screaming to the bus driver, *Get her!*

The potato beds are covered with raised dirt like fresh graves. Before quitting time, I raked over them to kill any early weeds. The cut seed potatoes are buried inside the mounds, and the fresh-tilled soil on top is so cool and soft and crumbly I want to lie down in it. Boss taught us this particular left-right sweeping motion to make, and I had almost figured out the rhythm when four o'clock came.

Got sixteen of twenty-three done and was disappointed; it's impossible to ever work fast enough. I told Boss how many I'd finished as I collected my things from my locker—he always has us stop working exactly on the hour to avoid overtime—and he said, Oh, did you?

At lunch, we found a stray husky dog in the barn eating cheese from Pena's lunch bag. Boss posted in the town Facebook group looking for its owner.

The owner came by after we all left, so Boss told us about it the next day. He never wastes time, but he did that morning, standing by our endless whiteboard checklist of things to weed, laughing. The man said the dog had likely escaped through the window of her (the dog's) bedroom, which he'd given her to keep her from mauling his pet fox. He didn't say where the fox slept at night. Also, the man added, he has put a pit bull in a headlock before.

I hear lots of stories from Boss and Kristy about "country people," who, the way they tell it, are different because they just don't know how to behave, like the man who crashed out of the woods on the farm's east end wearing only his underwear last fall, looked around at the two of them and the other crew members, and ran back into the trees, followed shortly by the police. They came to his house to bust him for selling fentanyl while he was in the shower and he ran for miles almost naked.

Boss jokes about how he's turning into a redneck out here without a wife to keep him civilized. He got divorced two years ago and now runs the farm alone. Other small houses line this shady dirt road, tucked back into the trees allowed to grow up through old fields, but he doesn't know who lives in them. He does everything in the city, where he came from.

The point in these stories, made clear and agreed upon though never said directly, is: We might be here right now, but we are not like them. Which feels so wrong to me, but I'm afraid to say so, because I can never convince myself I'm right about anything, or perhaps I don't want to be someone who thinks she knows better than someone else. I just suspect everything has a hidden dimension that will explain the problems away, and if I can't understand a situation, it's because I haven't found that secret yet. It has to make sense somehow; everybody must want to be good.

Anyhow, I don't feel this regional separation in myself, although I can't say why. I want the people who live out here to accept me though there's no reason why they should. When I go to the big white Wesco gas station up the road to buy a tamale in the middle of the day, I find myself scanning faces, trying to share a smile with someone. It's easy to create situations where you need to earn something.

Still trying to pinpoint what exactly about city living remains so important, other than that I was just told it somehow made me a more developed person. Right now, I feel the contrary, that my problems and my questions and all of my *feelings* come from a place of materially comfortable weakness. That comfort is a hard-won thing, though, too easy to disqualify when you were born into it yet not so simple to turn away from. I wonder if there's anything you can do to redeem yourself, become real again, once it's in you.

At home, someone else can always see me—even in my bedroom, because of the broken gap in the window blinds. Last night I listened to two men fighting outside and wondered what the big deal is about living in a place where there are "things to do," that phrase people use to explain why they fear the country.

Does human proximity, by nature, add value to a life? People seem to think so—even if the rest of the space in that life is used for evading others. We all do it, me sitting on the slide at the empty playground across the street after dark and Ryan's mother painting faces onto acorns in their basement and Sarah my Facebook roommate chopping salad in the dark.

I've thought for a long time that if I had any land of my own on which to do things, I would never feel bored or restless or unhappy, and I would never think to lament the limited supply of novelty gift stores within walking distance.

Plenty of things around me now, but where do I go? Still just the grocery store, mostly.

There's an undercurrent to my life of searching for a place where all of this viewing and performing and responding can stop, somewhere where we're all just standing upright.

Every morning, we:

roll up the plastic sides of the hoop houses with a hand crank to let the air in once the morning cold burns off

uncover the plants out in the fields, which we tucked in with white fabric the night before to keep them warm, holding it in place from the wind with shovelfuls of mud

write a checklist of tasks on the barn whiteboard

and run out of time to do everything we said we would.

Pena and I make sparse conversation, but when we talk, I feel like I have something to live up to. He only brings up church when Gwynn is listening. Discussing Mass in the early morning while sawing hunks of dill and securing them with rubber bands that leave tension marks on our hands, I remember things I've forgotten, like how I used to stand in front of that life-sized Jesus statue in church waiting and watching, how I couldn't turn away because I was completely certain the plaster was about to move.

Pena invited me to the bakery up the road from the farm at lunch and drove us there in his enormous, glistening new Ford truck. His parents bought it under the pretense of him paying them back, but now won't allow him. I wonder if they like him better than his four siblings or if they have changed their ways as their children grow old.

The Ford has air conditioning, unlike my car and apartment, and he told me I could sit in there to cool down after work. I think it's better that I don't get too used to the comfort. Riding into town, I got chills from the cold air against my sweat.

We ate peanut butter balls on the fraying wooden bench outside the bakery while he reviewed concepts in his nutrient management textbook, preparing for fall. At the other three corners of this intersection, the only one in town, are a restaurant, a hair salon, and an abandoned auto shop.

I worried Gwynn would be upset we had gone without her. Pena said on the drive back that he wanted to apologize. When he did, while we cut lettuce heads in the hoop house, she said defensively that she had been in her car anyway, on the phone with her boyfriend who was at the veterinarian for the ferret, whose tumors are inoperable.

Earlier she said the boyfriend got so drunk the night before that he fell into their bathtub and ripped the shower curtain rod out of the wall. Beer is his medicine, she said. She got upset at us for being concerned and embarrassing her with that kind of reaction.

Sometimes people seem to prefer it when you don't acknowledge your transgressions, would rather let the slight exist between you forever if making it right involves saying the thing out loud.

Later, Gwynn and I took so long trying to find enough salvageable chard leaves to hit our market quota that Boss sent Kristy to check on us. The beds are really diseased, big circles of dry brown blight on almost all the leaves except the tiny ones, and we have to save some of those because we harvest again for CSA in three days. Those without blight were chewed into lace by tiny snails we crush against the damp wooden siding of the hoop house with our shoes.

Our fingers were red prunes from snapping so many wet stems. You think you've looked through all the leaves, found every good one, but when you come up short, you go back and think the rest aren't that bad.

When Kristy opened the door to the hoop house to say What's going on in here? Gwynn turned to her with a fist full of rubber bands and the look of a snarling animal. Sometimes she seems so childlike that I forget she has some pretty impressive reservoirs of anger. She told me once that she cultivates her emotional youth on purpose as a rebellion against capitalism.

The market customers are scared of the vegetables. They ask with concern what they taste like, how I cook them, how I store them, what kind of nutrients are in an orange carrot versus a purple one. I'm not sad that they don't know, but rather that they are distant enough from the ground to care this much.

I suppose I have been distant too, physically speaking, but it always felt close to me, or a world that I understood at least. Then again, I have learned how to act like I've always been wherever I am.

There's just this kind of precious distance in the way most people approach us and smile with their gums showing. Novelty dominates their experience. There's a detachment in that, to take a selfie with a stack of lettuce heads you've never touched as if life is a source of props to capture a scene that you stage, like it's all just for you to *use.*

Nothing is really serious enough, but on the rare occasion I express this, people don't believe me, on account of my chipper disposition. I told Gwynn once that I don't like having fun and she laughed. Which I understand, because no matter what I'm feeling, I just can't stop smiling at everybody. I even laughed with her.

I did know that all of these ideas would trouble me—that farming and working on this scale can be a boutique endeavor. On the other hand, people need to eat. I don't know.

Watching couples and families walk by all afternoon gives

me this terrible longing sadness that I have to work hard to contain while looking out across the piles of salad bags and early onions and carrots left over from last fall. I try hard to believe in a version of myself who lives with sincere normalcy, who doesn't feel stuck or trapped by strange emotional prongs that keep me from fitting into anything just right. I'm convinced the first step to getting myself there is believing I can arrive, but I can't picture it, connect the idea to me. Same thing I felt in school when imagining a career.

Took a risk and shared this with Gwynn—only the part that seeing families with children makes me feel teary—and she said that she will not have a baby until we reverse climate change.

I came home to my empty apartment with its uneven wood floors and old windows painted shut and sat trembling on the couch for a few hours, looking at the cracks in the wall plaster. Sarah's car was gone and my neighbors' driveways were empty. We don't talk much, which I like most of the time.

I walked by my old church on Sunday morning and felt like there was something different about me that nobody knew or could see. For one thing, I'm sunburned and all my limbs are swollen up like a balloon animal's. But it's such a sedentary and quiet and clean place, you know?

I haven't gone inside the building since Easter Mass, when they set up tables in the back of the sanctuary selling carved wood ornaments and the homily urged us to do our duty to buy. I wanted to start screaming; my throat hurt from the pressure and I scraped a layer of skin off the backs of my hands with my fingernails, trying to make it go away. Every Sunday for years I'd felt tense and frightened and about to choke for a reason I couldn't understand. It sounds like nothing when I write it down.

I feel guilty about staying away; it's not something I'm relieved by. All through college I went to church every week on my own, sometimes twice, because if I say I believe in something I have to act accordingly, but now there is some almost physical barrier keeping me at home, looking at the ceiling. I ask every week to connect to something and rarely do. God isn't contained in a building or bureaucracy, but on the other hand, things do not seem to be resolving themselves as I go it alone.

Sometimes on my way home from work, I stop in other places, like the Wesco or the antique mall or the thrift stores that line the expanding suburbs, and feel I shouldn't be there because I have dirt all over myself, my shoes and my hands. It's surprisingly conspicuous just to be unclean somewhere.

Even though God lives in my every waking thought, I can't express a word about it to another person, can hardly write it down. It's covered within me, like one of those Mary statues shrouded by bathtubs that people here put in their front yards. Across the street from the church, one is set up outside a carport in an old basin that leaks rust down Mary's face.

Going to work is my first time being close to other religious people since my friend Allen and I fought last winter. I've forgotten how to justify my own silence. Allen and I had been glued to each other since the first day of college. He liked going to different churches together and taking pictures of the insides and talking about the music. I couldn't tell if it moved him or if he was just analyzing.

We fought over his boyfriend, whose stupidity and poor character and lack of depth he was always lamenting. After six months I said I didn't want to hear about it anymore if he wasn't going to act, which was something that took me a lot of time to work up the nerve to say. Allen laughed and said, Rawr! and made a catfight-type gesture with his hand, and then I wasn't afraid of what he thought about me anymore.

Small weeds grow fast between the onions and around the garlic, which was planted into straw last season. If you slice the weeds with a handheld hoe when they are young enough, they'll just up and die. For some reason, before, I thought plants would always re-root. A little bit less to fear.

Moved some row cover around, having an awful time keeping it from twisting in the wind. Gwynn told me unprompted that her boyfriend has a lot of trouble with who she is, with her not acting feminine anymore because she's deconstructing the religion that told her she had to, but he already moved across the country to be with her. What is the proper response? She has a real, serious relationship that has shaped years of her life; I've got a lot of people I'm loosely connected to circling around me, with less to talk about by the day.

Tiny and her boyfriend Shane are the only people I've seen since graduation. They're a few years older and more intense, mostly about politics, which makes me feel comfortable about not being much fun sometimes. The other groups I hung out with still invite me on day trips and bar crawls I don't have any energy for, and I feel bad about this because they make the effort to extend themselves, because they want me there, even though I get this feeling they really don't, on some deeper level they might not even be aware of.

One of them said to me a few months ago that all

these years she didn't even know I believed in God, said it to me like my faith being invisible was a great compliment, and it's been bothering me a lot. I wonder whether if I were dedicated more directly to the things I know have something behind them, at the expense of what is comfortable and right in front of me, my problems would change.

Sometimes at lunch, when we all eat together and stop moving around for the first time all day, I try to pray but find myself distracted by the nothingness I'd rather be thinking of.

I can only hope that I'll grow tired of pursuits that don't expect much from me in return.

Someone left a free office chair at the edge of a cornfield by the side of the road, and it's been there for weeks now, its sunken leather seat filled with water from the rain.

Every other morning, we harvest sweet peas, digging in the walls of vines between the strings and T-posts that hold them up off the moldy straw. The peas thicken into hard green pods the size of fingers. Between harvests, many become woody or spotted with brown divots.

When I was a baby, my mother called me Sweet Pea, and for some reason I feel the need to let everybody know this. I don't, but it's always ringing around there in the back of my mind.

Some of the folded thumbprint flowers are pink, a few purple, others white. I want them to smell like something, but I can't detect a scent. The straw makes us sneeze.

Pena and I worked together this morning, sharing a faded Rubbermaid harvest bin cracking into pieces around the sides where the handles once were. He invited me to a badminton game for religious youth at his older sister's apartment complex out in the marsh beyond the west side of the city.

I can't picture myself attending. I'm not a religious youth, am I? The people at the church groups I tried in school seemed so far away that I came to think of myself as something else. You're taught that it's weak and wrong to stop attending because of other people, but you can only go to so many meetings feeling like an alien, like you're not normal enough for God to touch.

Pena doesn't have friends (he's never met anyone he

wasn't related to who was worth knowing—he said that), so it is probably a significant offering, which will make it worse if I say no. I told him that I am worried about the way my fingers have been popping out of their joints, but I'll let him know. I'm trying to overrride the impulse to think that the difference between us means one of us is doing right more than the other.

Last night I watched a movie about cowboys and imagined scrambling around in a gully or a ditch like I used to as a kid. There's some tiny bit of childlike novelty in spending the days engaged with dirt again. It's so humid in the mornings here that you sweat the moment you stand up.

I learned from Red over the phone a few months ago that biting into an apple can stop you crying when you eat something too spicy. Nobody had ever told me that before.

I used to talk on the phone a lot more than I do now. I haven't learned anything that way in a while. When I mention Sweet Pea to my mother, she remembers it as a relic—*Well, that was when you were a baby.*

This is not cold, only factual. She has suffered through so much that she doesn't know how to be warm and fuzzy.

I don't really want to play badminton. I don't want to meet anyone new, or begin anything else; I haven't figured out how to manage what I have. I don't want to say no to anything in the world, either. Maybe that's the problem.

The chance remains that everything will change. If anything changes, it will not change today, which is all that I can live through. I could sneeze at the movie and slice something up from the core.

Two of the farm cats had kittens this week, and when I left today Kristy was crouched underneath her car holding one of them in the palm of her hand. The kittens don't have their eyes open yet; I'm not sure how that one got away from its mother. Boss warns us to check our tires and wheel wells for stowaways every day.

Kristy said that every year Boss refuses to get the cats fixed but won't explain why, and all the kittens die by autumn. The one she held was orange and white. I turned around when I saw her there and went back into the barn like I had forgotten something.

Used the post hole digger to make homes for one hundred and eighty cucumber plants in the sixth hoop house. The digger has a pair of rounded metal blades attached to two long wooden handles, which you drive into the ground over and over, then pinch together to lift the dirt out. The ground is packed hard here, and the cucumbers need a decent depth, so it took about seven or eight slams into the ground for each one.

Didn't hurt too much, and I was surprised to discover my body being useful. I'm so used to criticizing how it looks that I forget it serves a purpose. Pena started on the digger and then walked over quietly and asked me to help. It's taller than him, and he can't get the leverage he needs to cut into the dirt, like a child wrestling with a pair of stilts.

Kristy followed behind us, scooping soil supplement pellets into the holes with a disintegrating Styrofoam cup, and said that anyone who cared about their employees would dig with a motorized auger instead. She tells tales of all kinds of small farm machinery we will never have: transplanting machines, potato conveyor belts, ride-behind harvesters.

I'm less sore from lifting the digger than from feeling the shocks in my bones that the blades made when they hit the ground.

A photo of me shoveling compost made it in the newsletter, but my dad didn't want to send it to my grandmother. My parents are confused about what I'm doing but say they trust it. Grandma, meanwhile, believes that because we are women, it was never our lot to labor in the first place. I feel even more sick and scared than usual imagining my life ending up like hers, which she has spent in her living room. I tell her about work and she says, Don't they have any men there to do that for you?

We transplanted all the nightshades (tomatoes, peppers, tomatillos) and cucurbits (winter and summer squash, pumpkins, red and yellow fleshed watermelons, cantaloupes) to the field today—more than an acre of produce. The cucurbits went into holes we ripped with our hands in sheets of thin black plastic, then buried into place with a tractor attachment. The sheets will keep the weeds off when their vines get too thick for us to reach the dirt.

Boss drove the tractor with his new yellow noise-cancelling headphones, which also play wireless music. He showed us at lunch yesterday. Every time he stopped, Kristy would yell out to ask what he was listening to. He likes Beyoncé.

Because we are supposed to move as fast as we possibly can all the time, there is often this competitive feeling running underneath everything, though I don't know if everyone else is aware of it or if I have some kind of chip on my shoulder. I think I'm not used to learning new things; I survived with the same basic set of abilities for all the years I spent in school.

Kristy is always watching, and I often know exactly how long it will take for her to come correct me. I'm tempted to give up on trying to find the right way to do things on my own. We're not allowed to listen to music when we work, of course, but somehow it's different on the tractor.

I'm getting obsessive about the state of my hands, particularly along the sides of my pointer fingers, which are permanently caked with dirt in the existing ridge-and-valley pattern of the skin there. No matter how much I scrub them, they never look clean.

We bring in different lotions and salves and balms to try after we wash our hands at the end of the day and none of them work. The skin cracks and peels and rasps like sandpaper. When I untangle my hair, the breaking skin catches against my scalp. Standing long enough to scrub the dirt off the rest of me at home often feels like the most difficult thing I've ever done or dreamed of. Taking a cold shower after coming in from the heat actually makes you hotter (What? Kristy says so). Most nights I go to bed at six or seven.

Last night Red texted me a photo of a can of beans sitting casually on the handrail in his building's elevator.

The realest and most important part of my life is the drive through the country to the farm every morning and afternoon. In part, this is because I am addicted to the feeling of going somewhere, but also just being out of the city, seeing open ground, makes me think about pulling my station wagon over and launching myself into the grass and lying down.

The desire to leave, to see something new, has become a shameful one, like how searching outwards is the mark of an underdeveloped spirit. I act as if other people will think the same of me if I admit this. I've already started taking different roads because the ones I started on are familiar, don't hold as much to see.

Two routes take the same amount of time: one through these fields, past the dairy farms and dissolving barns and the ridge lined with an array of antique tractors, or a straight shot on the state highway along miles of tract housing. Beyond the guardrail, a lake sits surrounded by bars in low wooden buildings that look like set pieces from Western movies. I don't know anyone who lives there.

Today I took the state road home, not trusting myself to make it through all the turns of the country roads, and stopped at a grocery store built in a new subdivision with homes radiating out from its parking lot. I didn't pack enough for lunch because I was too tired to cook last night and ended up with a kind of hunger I never knew before this, one that makes all my muscles twinge.

The store was empty, and so was the parking lot and the manufactured lake, and while spending almost twenty minutes inside to leave only with a jar of peanut butter that I ate in my car off of a plastic knife, I couldn't help thinking that this little place had to be a dead one.

I can't explain this any better—I know disqualifying suburbia is played out, and it's not premised on anything intellectual, just this feeling I had watching one lone high schooler running along the shoulder of the road and dropping at the stop sign to do push-ups, his sweat darkening a sidewalk so clean that he could have been the first person to ever touch the ground there.

Gwynn wanted to talk about heaven while we transplanted Brussels sprouts in bed 9C, facing the woods. I carried the trays and dropped wet seedling blocks to the dusty ground for her to pick up and pop into the holes made by the dibbler. We soak the seedlings in diluted fish waste fertilizer mix before transplanting, to help them survive the shock, and it leaked all over me, stinking worse the longer the sun shone on it and then burning off into nothing.

It felt strange to watch from above as Gwynn scrambled around with the dirty seedlings I dropped onto her hands. The Brussels sprouts are spindly and small, an inch or two high, with tiny purple leaves that flutter like banners on their descent. How do you know it's real? she asked me.

It frightens me when people ask me what I think because there is always so much going on. I can't run through anything I say, be sure that it's true or that there is a good reason for me to say it. It doesn't help that I don't experience much of anything in words. At the same time, it feels like a waste to experience what I do and be unable to share with other people who want it.

Maybe I don't understand life enough yet; I'm hoping that's the reason. Hey, man, sorry, I'm just not ready. I told her the truth, that the faith I know focuses more on what we do here than what might surprise us after.

Gwynn said she was traumatized in childhood by being told about Hell. That surprised me; I remember finding comfort in the thought that it mattered what we did, like they told us in all those different church basements while my parents were trying to find something to fix them. Something had to matter. She's trying to unlearn the idea.

I got: two hands, one heart, all that, a bushel of garlic, sore ankles, a Japanese cucumber Ryan grew on his neighbor's land without asking, a spinach croissant, and a pint of concord grapes at market today.

Then I got so excruciatingly lonely afterwards, like every Saturday afternoon. I come back to my empty apartment exhausted and full of this biting need for something *more more more* to go out with, to come home to. Maybe it's seeing so many people in one day. I drank a beer and gnashed my teeth. I know I'm just starting out in life, but it's often hard to believe anything else will ever happen. I can barely think in the evenings.

Snapped the scapes off every garlic plant today, the spiraling, woody green stems growing from their tops that would open into flowers if we left them to live. Instead, their energy goes down to the bulbs. The broken insides coat your hands with a slick gel that smells of industrial dinners; the moldering straw around the bases of the plants, which kept them warm all winter, makes you sneeze.

My face swelled up from it and I felt ugly. But who cares? The clear plastic bags with holes punched in their sides were filled, twist-tied shut and staked in the cooler by two in the afternoon.

Everyone's going to ask you what you do with these, at market, Boss said, and you're going to tell them you make a delicious pesto.

Used up the afternoons this week pruning tomatoes, which fill a whole hoop house. Wretched hot. They're growing almost twelve inches a week. The seedlings were planted in the first week of the season, their limbs secured with plastic clips to twine hung from cables across the top of the hoop house. Every other week we clip their new lengths to the stained white plastic strings. We cut off the suckers, or new shoots, from the elbows of the plants with tiny gummed-up scissors so they can focus their energies on their fruits, rather than growing larger.

Kristy and Boss fought about whether we should also pinch off every other little yellow flower to make the plants focus even further. Kristy lost after Boss loudly reminded her who signs her paychecks. The pointy, lacy leaves look like they should hurt when you brush against them, but they don't.

The plants let out a tar-like substance that builds up on our fingers. The tar doesn't come off with soap, either; Pena said he washes his hands in vinegar at home. I can almost imagine him filling up a claw foot tub with plastic jugs of Heinz distilled white.

Kristy and I were talking while we worked—I forget what about, already—and I said offhand, Yeah, I feel things and I understand them, and she wanted to know how I came up with these "ideas."

Oh, I was just thinking about it this morning, I said, or something boneless like that.

She asks a lot of questions that I don't like to answer, because they feel pointed toward a conclusion she is trying to draw, unlike Gwynn's, which are just asking directly for all that we have. It's also hard to think while working as fast as you can in a plastic room that's a hundred and eight degrees.

Wonder how it's so easy for other people to communicate with each other. We work together all day and talking never ends. I've told my coworkers about my boiled-egg roommate, my friends whose lives are in freefall, my high school drinking, my unsettling neighbors. My family is the one subject I can avoid; I've already learned to be quiet about them, already know how much I can't explain.

In a quiet moment, Gwynn said that in a perfect world she'd spend all day "lovin' on" plants like this, where she can pay extreme, excruciating attention to detail. I'm more into the little half-aprons from Home Depot, stained beyond recognition from yellow-green tar, that hold our plastic clips. Garb for tomato artisans. Working slowly down the rows of plants, you start to feel you know them. It's a similar thing with the branches arching over the road on the drive home. Even though each is a different variety, we make a competition out of whose pruning will produce the most fruit.

For all the effort I expend to express myself perfectly through all this, I leave each day feeling deeply embarrassed, overextended, and freakish. Does life feel this difficult to everyone? Sped by the pasture ten minutes from the farm with no animals in it except a horse and a small donkey, and today the donkey was facing the horse's side with his head resting against its flank, neither of them moving except for their tails.

We've moved our start time up half an hour because the sunrise comes earlier than it used to. The day breaks in half over the kale.

Haven't heard from Red at all this month. As I harvest, I think about him because the existence of whatever we did share, confusing as it is, gives me more hope than most other things in my life. The last time I saw him before he moved, we went on a walk to identify grass species in the ravines, which no one else knows how to appreciate even though the place is open to the public in the middle of the city. He was wearing this black and white windbreaker from high school that barely fit his shoulders.

Representative?! —No!

Is this desire for clarity *now* instead of waiting for things to be revealed a failure of conviction?

Red used to go to church too and enrolled in seminary after high school, before I knew him, but at confession one day the priest made a comment on his sins that was so terrible Red never went back. I wonder if he respects me less for still being tangled up like this. I'm not sure why my relationship with faith is so colored by the fear of it hurting other people.

On Saturdays I used to leave Red's day-drinking hangouts for afternoon Mass at the old church up the street, then walk back and stay until one or two in the morning.

I did this every weekend for almost a year, but none of the people at his house became my friends too. I felt I was embarrassing him somehow, but each week I thought I could be better and fix the week before, and he kept inviting me. Sometimes I wondered what they talked about when I left, whether they said things like Tiny's old boyfriend, who told her he would be interested in me except I reminded him too much of his little sister.

The last time I went to Red's, I didn't eat anything before church and had a mystical experience watching an ant crawl over the back of a pew and a daughter pick a strand of hair off her mother's sweater while the organ wheezed. Every piece of light in the sanctuary was holding something. When I returned to the house I told Red about it, watching him pour a freshly cracked Guinness in the kitchen, and he said something like Well, you know you made that happen, you manufactured the conditions for it, but I'm sure it probably still counts if it felt real to you.

I went outside and his dumb friend Atheist Geoff said to me on the porch, You're smoking after the Eucharist? Wow, really nice, and in addition to my shame about that, it shocked me to think that maybe some people don't question whether God is real, they just don't care either way.

Sometimes on Tuesday mornings I'm in an awful mood, coming back into work again, having lost momentum by sitting on the front steps for two days. We start those mornings with kale harvest for the CSA; we've got the thick scaly kind and the thin type with tightly wound curls at its edges that slice our hands like paper cuts. The plants fan out in crowns of leaves around knee height and are soaking wet with dew in the morning. Boss has waterproof PVC overalls we can wear, but I never do because they don't breathe at all, and it's hard to feel yourself move.

It hurts to bend my fingers, not because my muscles are sore, but because of some swelling or resistance I can't understand the source of.

I feel dissatisfied by most everything I look at, but I'm still working out how to wrangle the things I can't see into an order that builds toward something. It's almost too obvious to be worth saying, I guess, but I'm surprised how much of life seems a choice between comfortable boredom and grasping blindly toward a light so bright it could make you blind.

The peas are increasingly woody and brown, more voles are chewing on them, and the plants use their own weight to slip free of the twine that holds them upright. There's constant calculus on the farm of your input time and your output yield, which determines whether to search for good peas to harvest, restring them between their posts, weed below them, trap the voles, et cetera. Everything you do, every second of your day, can be broken down into outcomes and cents and future stability. So we abandon the peas, which are not particularly profitable anyhow, and I miss them like a friend once that patch of field is tilled under and planted with clover to restore the nutrients they took to grow.

It's funny (and by that, I mean it makes me feel crazy) when people from college act like this is some cute activity I'm doing because I'm burned out or tired of working on anything "meaningful."

Dr. L even said that to me across his desk before I graduated. He said, You'll come back in here next year and we'll talk grad school after you've had your break. In my mind then, I could see a series of people in various doorways swatting me with file folders all the way down into Hell.

If it weren't for him, I might have left school altogether, without anyone to show me conventional things could be deep and challenging and I myself was capable of digging into them. I said I'm not doing this to run from anything, and even if I find out it's not forever, I won't regret the time I spent with it. He made a little amused face.

As my mom pointed out, it would make him look good if I got into a good school. She doesn't trust anyone's intentions, and naturally I'm the opposite (it's myself I don't trust), but life seems to prove her right. Later, she said maybe she was wrong, maybe they are just worried I'm making survival more difficult than it needs to be. One of my other professors said her *dream* was for me to go to Syracuse and create beautiful maps. Her dream—I want to cry just thinking about it. As difficult as all of this is, I still don't feel I've made a mistake.

I saw Dr. L at market, which I guess is what's making me dissect this again. It doesn't really matter—it's my life, and I'm the one who has to live with it—but I wish we could be in on it together, me and all the people I care about.

My old friend Anita, who I hadn't seen since she got that boyfriend three years ago and we told her we were worried about how much he ordered her around and she stopped speaking to all of us, walked by the market stall the week before last. We accidentally made eye contact, so she had to stop and make the necessary small talk.

Looking at her, spooky blonde vegan Anita who I was never close to but shared life with anyway in a time of starting over, I missed her so much that I desperately meant the polite chatter. I needed to know what she had been up to and how wedding planning was going and if she liked her job managing aquatic plant restoration projects, so much that I almost wanted to cry. I don't know if she knew I was serious about how glad I was she stopped. It seems good words are hard to say in a way that people will believe.

Is this like your summer thing? she asked, smiling distantly like you would at someone else's child.

Freshman year, six of us cut class to camp up north in the middle of the week, crammed in a tent in the rain sharing her giant Tupperware of vegan peanut butter balls. The shape of that life reappeared then and pressed onto me for the rest of the day. We had met carpooling to clean trash off the riverbanks with a school group. Sitting in Anita's back seat, watching her talk to my other future friend Anne about water pollution, I had thought it was alright if we never crossed paths again; I was just glad they existed and that I knew about it.

At market she didn't buy anything. She'd already

gotten some carrots. See ya later, she said, and disappeared into the crowd.

The spinach and arugula and salad mixes had started to sweat in their plastic bags as the sun moved toward us. Gwynn and I shook the bags one by one to redistribute the condensation inside so the leaves would be visible again. We did a little dance with them as we went and Ryan shook his head.

He took a metal key from his pocket and turned on the faucet head built into one of the permanent awning's metal support beams so we could wet the carrots, which were going limp in the heat; he said he stole the key from one of the former market coordinators because he got sick of asking for help. The water came out with the force of an emergency, and it almost hurt our dry hands to hold the carrots under them, to bring them back to life.

I'm trying to say that I feel hopeful, I'm trying to say it just like that, because hope to me is in all our human disasters, how we know enough of the good thing to wreck ourselves in its absence.

Still emotional, I texted Anne that I had seen Anita and that she seemed okay. Anne invited me to a cookout with some of her boyfriend's friends and his family at their lake house the next day. I decided I would go, to connect with some selfhood outside the farm, and also because Anne gets upset when I say no, which I always do since I'm so tired and stiff it's hard to walk or smile. She needs people to be intensely committed to her, to prove something, while I'm scared of their complexity and my inability to remain myself around them. I know how to show up and be diligent and generally available, but there's this internal wall I get stuck behind. I think she can sense this, and it has only caused problems for us.

Most of our old friend group has drifted away toward their jobs or boyfriends or futures. One of them told me before he moved away that Anne always (always!) complained to him bitterly that I thought I was better than her. I couldn't look him in the eyes afterward; it's so difficult even to write it down. The biggest sin of many that I failed to overcome, identified by my own best friend, who said nothing but kept inviting me in, hating me when I didn't show up and hating me more when I did.

I still want to fix it. Try again and do it better this time. Quitters get nowhere.

We stood around in the soggy grass by the lake holding sweating beer bottles while a procession of Anne's boyfriend's relatives pointed and laughed at the startling clarity of the tan lines I have developed on my ankles from the tick-resistant treated socks I wear to work. Her boyfriend was playing cornhole with friends of his father's, looking hearty. Watching everyone make their motions, this tender grasping feeling struck my heart, which happens sometimes and might be a real spiritual moment or just my own made-up significance, who can say.

Weeding and weeding. The rows where we planted the pumpkins were a grass pathway last year and although Boss has tilled it up half a dozen times since then, the grass still grows. The pumpkin vines are long and spiky and we have to crawl under them to get at the grass underneath. Hurts a lot.

Gwynn, who loves animals, found a toad and picked it up; everyone yelled at her to go wash her hands and acted disgusted for the rest of the morning. I never knew that you could catch a disease from a toad, but apparently there are many. The crew treated her passion as an act of biological warfare. Pena pulled me aside at lunch and said he worried that something was seriously wrong with her. I don't know what I should do, or how to talk to her about it, he said as we tied our aprons to prune the tomatoes again.

Gwynn was not ashamed, and posted the toad on Instagram later. I know because last week she followed my account from inside the steamy portable toilet with the wasp living in it that faces our lunch table—she went in, and I got the notification before she came out.

I went over to see Shane and Tiny after work and we sat on their porch, sweating and listening to Jeopardy! through the open window with the busted screen that lets bugs inside. Shane always has the TV on, every day and every night, which usually I hate, but over there it feels okay because of its consistency. The open wound of the human world is always in front of us anyway, so might as well turn the sound on and look at the pictures.

He decapitated a Hamm's beer with a can opener and we had to yell at him not to drink it; he said he could avoid the metal shards, filter them through his teeth like a whale. We didn't talk about much.

On the way to my car, I had to stand with my hand against a tree and throw up for at least five minutes. I don't know why. I felt fine before, and only had one drink, and no metal shards to eat, no toads in my hands.

I drove to the Wesco at lunch after a morning scrubbing harvest bins and bought a tamale wrapped in melting plastic. My hands were raw and smelled of hydrogen peroxide; my knees locked with the cold stiffness of wash day. Sat in the parking lot and ate with the radio on, thinking about whether I could find somewhere to buy whitewall tires for my wagon. It was on my mind because the only station I like out here plays that one Billy Joel song all the time.

Watched a man get out of his truck who, honest, looked exactly like Humpty Dumpty, wearing a pair of knee britches (including suspenders) with a large and very visible shitstain running all the way up the seat. He carried a half-full sixty-four-ounce soda bottle and was shouting hoarsely at the young boy with him.

I filed this away to tell my coworkers, and then I wondered if collecting and retelling anecdotes about other people is actually a form of cruelty. Most of these images point towards something else that I don't have the words for, this kind of larger narrative in life, so I try to approximate what I think it all means by illustrating, but I fear that underneath I am just trying to laugh.

I don't like it when I think about myself too much, and I don't like it when I think about other people too much either. It seems harder than it should be to just experience something simply. Even when I talk to God, it's usually over what I should do about earthly things. That's something I have to remember to do; it feels like physically lifting my mind upwards, and my arms hurt.

The idea I had was that working with my hands would diminish the number of thoughts I had on human subjects, but instead they're all I can think about, being the parts of the world that are real and right in front of me.

On my way back to the farm, the old man mowing the old roadside cemetery waved from among its big white crosses. Imagine resting all the time like that and imagine realizing you hadn't done all you could while on earth. It's hard to work now, but one day you'll miss being able to. Consider this in hindsight, which it will soon be. That's what I told myself as I crouched down in the dirt, feeling sick from tamale grease and artificially flavored raspberry tea.

We spent the rest of the day hacking at grass clods with trowels and ripping lamb's quarter from the ground with our hands. The onions are getting tall. The garlic's already starting to brown, and the zucchini produces ten thousand new woody fruits every day. We transplanted a few of the seedlings too late and they went into the ground slightly lopsided, so they grow sideways and flower inconsistently.

In four hours, we pulled every garlic plant from the ground. We bundled them with twine and hung them from the rafters of the old barn to dry. Once they're ready to store, we'll get to spend a whole morning sitting down to clip the long tops from the bulbs. Kristy stood on the ladder hanging the plants as we brought them to her; she found initials carved into the tops of the old beams by whoever had built the barn.

Wouldn't it be nice if we could just harvest all the time? Gwynn said so, and Pena said maybe, but he doesn't like garlic very much. It's an unnecessary crop, too intensely flavored.

It's warm enough now that we don't need to cover the more sensitive plants each night. Only the Brussels sprouts remain blanketed, to protect them from the flea beetles eating pin-sized holes in the leaves. If there's any breeze at all, the fabric twists and tangles as you try to pull it across the rows, like making a giant's dirty bed in a wind tunnel.

Kristy rigged up a new system to store the fabric for fall. Before, it was folded into awkward, bulky pillows stuffed haphazardly in the old barn. Most of the beds are different lengths, requiring specific sections of fabric that were difficult to find and full of spiders. This time we taped one end of the fabric to a PVC pipe balanced between two sawhorses and used a hand crank stuck in the end of the pipe to roll it up. It worked perfectly and fast.

Kristy was smiling. I've been trying to get him to let me do this for years, she said to us absently, meaning Boss, And I have so many more ideas like this.

She wiped her forehead with the back of her hand, her face starting to look pinched.

Today it was my turn to drive into the farm before sunrise, pick up the vegetable van, and drive it back to town for market. Gwynn has been doing it every week even though we were supposed to be switching off. She kept saying she didn't want to put that pressure on me, and I told her that if I say I don't mind I mean I don't mind, but it made no difference. It was nice of her to do, but some part of me is afraid it was because she thinks I need help. I got to drive this time because she had to take her ferret to the vet again and could only find an appointment that afternoon.

I liked getting up at four and driving in the dark. It had that special childhood-vacation feeling, making coffee with the lights on in the dark and moving down an empty yellow highway. Once I got out into the country everything plunged back into black. Minute to minute, it lightened again over the houses and the trees and the long grass moving in the wind against my headlights.

Something about the newness of it all against that familiar ground got me emotional. A Procol Harum song on the AM oldies station actually made me cry. Mice chewed through half the car's radio wires a decade ago, so I have to hit the dashboard sometimes to make the sound come into focus. I passed the crystal shop and the car repair barn and a woman jogging down the road in reflective pants.

Thought about all this love I never quite get to, all the emotional near-misses of my life and the events that never really seem to alter me like they do other people, like

Gwynn catching her toad or Ryan sleeping in his van up north or Red holding a trout, feeling it breathe in his researching hands. I'm so close to everything but never touch it. Maybe it's because I'm too afraid, but what I can do if my fear has guarded me through life?

After that I felt nothing at all.

At the farm, Boss whistled while we packed up in the dark, sliding bins and trays into the dirt-caked carpet on the floor of the vegetable van. He knows how to arrange everything so it fits right in.

Go get em! And don't worry about the engine light, it's always on, he said when we finished, slapping the van like it was a horse's flank.

The van rattles and bounces and wheezes and accelerates almost too easily and has an excellent stereo system. It doesn't have a rearview mirror or a camera, so Ryan waved me through a twenty-point turn to back into our market stall while cars and trailers lined up impatiently. Sometimes I think he likes me, but mostly I think he thinks I'm stupid. Either that or he can tell how much everything matters to me.

You really need to get better at this, he said unpleasantly as I started unloading beet crates. Then he showed me a tooth that fell out of his mouth and into his hand last night while he foraged for mushrooms in the park next to the house he squats in when his mom needs space. The tooth was chipped in the front from a kernel of heritage corn he grew on a traffic island, dried in his van, and then bit down too hard on a few years ago.

His palm is tattooed with the faint streaky face of a flaming cross. Last week he told an inquiring customer that the cross doesn't signify anything because it's upside down, and when I looked over, he said coldly that he wasn't talking to me.

This time, he pushed his lip up with his finger to show me the raw bloody gap where the tooth had been. Go on, touch it, he said. The market didn't open for another hour, but customers were already pacing the concrete in front of us to get zucchini and radicchio and spinach before it sold out, anxiously clutching their empty tote bags.

Seeing Anne again had given me a new drive to redeem myself, a conviction that I really was strong enough to be the way I feel I should be around people, so I agreed to camp with her and a few other old friends and nine of her boyfriend's frat brothers after market.

I worked the stand alone. More people than usual complained that the produce was too expensive, and I ran out of plastic bags, and Ryan turned cold again and left without saying goodbye, and one woman actually asked if there was an adult who could help me when I messed up the mental math making change for her. I wanted to flake and lie on the floor for the rest of the day.

Finally alone in my ninety-five-degree room after driving the van back to the farm and then my car back to my apartment, my feet up against the wall with the squirrel scratching inside it and my eyes burning, I felt so sick of myself and my sensitivity to other people and my fixation on my own flaws and all of these *thoughts* and *feelings* in place of simple action that I got out of bed and put my shoes back on.

I worried a bit about the car, because I had never

driven it that far before, but I was sick of being afraid, too. The two-hour drive went by easy; I had the window down and the radio on, I read all the billboards for cheap burials and weed stores and watched the sky turn pink. Ten minutes away from the campsite, alone on a country road, my station wagon threw itself to a stop with a screeching, crunching sound and wouldn't move anymore.

I put it in neutral and pushed it off onto the shoulder, something I hadn't known I knew how to do. Under the hood it hissed like an animal. Whatever was crunching inside made a horrible screeching sound and resisted my arms, the muscles twitching in them, the stiff bracing of my knees against the cold metal. It smelled of plastic burning at a distance. The birds sang and the crickets chirped in the hayfields on either side of us. I was afraid it would explode if I pushed it further.

Then I called Anne and walked a hundred feet down the road in case the car burst into flames. It was quiet under the trees; I faced a small cemetery and had one of those brief detached pockets of time when I feel like nothing bad has ever happened to me or ever will.

By the time Anne's car pulled up, I was about to cry and couldn't relax because whatever I had done now seemed unfixable and far-reaching. I had not focused on any of the right things, I had been wrong to invest myself into proving something through human relationships, I had wasted so much time trying to change myself and other people and the path of my life with the sheer force of my own personal will, I knew the trip was a bad idea but made it anyway, and now I was trapped with the consequences.

I wished I was at home again so I could close myself

in my room and do nothing but wait for God to tell me what to do. Of course no one can do anything by themselves. Didn't I already know that? *Please help me*, I thought, hating how feeble and predictable it was to ask for help after a mistake I knew I'd make.

Anne brought her boyfriend and our old friend Nate, who stumbled out of the backseat to hug me too long and too tightly. His face smelled like Mike's Hard Lemonade and vaporized marijuana. We once had a lot of fun together, spending entire weekends driving around and sitting in the park and running errands. His good nature was still there, but he seemed to be aging backwards, and I barely knew how to talk to him anymore.

I pushed him off me and said What is the matter with you.

I'm so happy you're here, he said with his eyes closed, smiling. But now you'll have to pay me to pick you up. Friendship isn't free.

He put his arms around me and laughed. Calm down, everything's fine, it's fine.

Then I couldn't help it, I yelled at him for trying to make it a joke, for being drunk all the time and not listening to me and never acting serious. Stop it, stop it, I kept saying while trying to squirm away, it's not funny.

He just laughed and tightened his grip like he'd never been happier, and I pushed against him with my forearms and kept yelling, but he seemed not to even hear me or feel me moving. Up close, he smelled of Old Spice and stale tobacco and sweating horses. I wanted to slap him to make him quit it, which scared me. I felt small and futile realizing that I could have been screaming at everybody all along instead of being so obsessively careful about my behavior and it wouldn't have made a difference.

Finally Anne pulled Nate back into her car and closed the door behind them. He went easily when she led him. I put my hands over my eyes and stopped crying. For once, I didn't apologize.

Her boyfriend, who is very nice and steadfast and looked afraid, poked around under the hood of my station wagon while I stood behind him feeling morose. He admitted he didn't know what was wrong and we left it on the side of the road to spend the night alone.

I haven't lost it in front of anybody I wasn't related to before. It feels like something I can't come back from. I called my parents to tell them, and their voices were stiff. In the backseat of Anne's Corolla, where everybody was probably thinking about how I had turned out to be *way too much after all, really not a good person*, Nate flopped his head on my shoulder and said I'm sorry in this baby-like voice.

I wanted to grab his blond hair and pull it all out, hold him down and shave his patchy beard right off him. I wanted to make him angry, make him take me seriously enough to get pissed at. I wanted to know what had happened to him and to all of us and how much it really mattered. I wanted to know if any of it could be fixed, if it was ever all right to stop trying. I wanted to know why everything is so difficult and why I have such a hard time, even though I've accepted difficulty and I'm not afraid of it.

The campground was in the center of a small town, across from two competing gas stations, and children in camper vans screamed around us almost all night.

We swam in the lake and roasted marshmallows and everything. I tried to smile and felt like a fraying maniac, a pretender. One of the frat brothers brought a head of cabbage for the planned taco dinner and called it lettuce. Before I could catch myself, I said Wait, that's cabbage, and everyone looked at me. Know-it-all! Nate went home after midnight for his opening shift at Best Buy.

The tent was too cold to sleep in. If I prayed, I knew I'd start crying, and I didn't want Anne to hear and think it was because I didn't like her.

Got the car towed in the morning and found out the alternator exploded, which would cost four times its value to fix. Now I can't go anywhere on my own. Kristy and I will need to carpool. Somehow, I feel relieved, maybe because I drove the car for so long it had become part of who I was.

Frat Brother Bryce gave me a ride home. Turns out we are almost neighbors. He has an unfinished look about him, like he was born sitting down and never got up, with this bashful-hound-dog affect in his dark eyes. He said that they were waiting for me to arrive the day before because Nate behaved better when I was around. Anne and her boyfriend want me in their eventual wedding for this reason, he said.

I don't want to be a negative person, but the things people do just upset me so much sometimes.

Bryce stopped for an extra-large strawberry milkshake at a Wendy's in one of the fringe suburbs that stretch on forever. I was feeling penitential and out of control and wanted to deny myself something, so I lied about having plans for lunch later and watched him slurp it in the parking lot, which was newly paved and smelled like the guts of the earth.

While eating the cherry off the end of his straw, he told me he orders this exact milkshake at least every other day because he is always going through something that leads him to deserve one.

Kristy and I carpooled in silence on Tuesday, arriving early so she could prepare a plan to fit the carrots we were about to harvest into the overflowing cooler room. While she slammed things around on the other side of the refrigerated steel door, I bagged salad greens Boss had cut over the weekend because it got so hot they were in danger of bolting and repeated to myself that everything was *fine.*

Inside the hoop house it got up to a hundred degrees by ten o'clock, even though we had the sides rolled all the way up. The vent fan is jammed and nobody has time to fix it. Sweat rolled down our foreheads and burned in our eyes.

I like how tall the carrot greens grow, the little dense forest they make. We needed to clear them out to make room for more radishes. The field carrots still aren't ready, so we will go without them at market for a week or two.

The carrots had been in the ground so long and were planted together so closely that the greens grew into a mat of wet mold that fell right off into the aisle when we raked over them. Usually, they're thinned out once they sprout, but there wasn't enough time this spring.

Had to use a pitchfork to dig up the bald roots, which somehow were fine, and rubber band around the base instead. I twist the tops off for customers anyway, who ask anxiously if they will be composted, to which I am instructed to lie and say yes. Some of them will ask if there's anything to use them for, and I am supposed to tell them about carrot top pesto. Everything is pesto. Everything is pesto, and I need to be locked away somewhere.

I felt flat and strange and unsettled and wanted to just keep digging down in that irrigation-wet dirt until I could hit clay and stop being myself. I hadn't heard from anyone since Sunday. Working almost felt good, finally, having something to do that was some other, outside kind of feeling. For a while, I decided, I won't make time for anything else.

The ground was wet where the greens had kept the sun from getting in, and the knees of our pants soon had an inch of mud built up. Kristy will eat carrots right off the pitchfork. She bit a purple one and joked about its higher vitamin content.

She planted them in the winter. She's the only year-round employee, although Boss just gives her part-time hours until March, so she makes up the difference delivering pizzas. She said the seeder broke, so she and Boss were planting the whispery little carrot seeds by hand, the whole hoop house worth, but about fifteen minutes in he got up to get some water and never came back for the rest of the day.

Kristy told him later that she was upset, that he was not treating her fairly, and he said that was what the money was for. Like the line from *Mad Men*, because all he does outside of work is watch prestige television shows on a big screen mounted to a wall of the farmhouse, so he only knows how to think about other people as opportunities to win.

While we were pulling weeds around the lettuce heads a few weeks ago, she told me that if she ever stopped farming, she would probably kill herself.

Later, while harvesting a very early row of potatoes because we'd lost an entire lettuce planting to slugs and needed something else for CSA, Boss cut a vole in half with the digger attachment on the tractor. I accidentally put my hand right into it while sifting through the dirt. This upset Gwynn so much she had to go sit down in the drainage gully at the end of the field.

To harvest, the digger opens up the row, making a valley of the middle, and we sift for the potatoes embedded in these dirt walls, crawling with crates alongside us and dropping the potatoes in as we find them. Boss was working across from me when I found the vole, scrabbling through his side of the valley. He stood up and stomped its bones flat with his boot to make sure it was dead. I rubbed my hand in the dirt to get the blood off.

Everybody seemed angry with Gwynn for crying and wasting time. She is stubborn about honoring her feelings, no matter what they are. I wonder if this has to do with her work at unlearning Hell.

It's the facts of life, Kristy and Boss said to her, as if knowledge always leads to acceptance.

The first cherry tomatoes are ready in the hoop house, the big slicing varieties not far behind them. These little ones grow from the end of each branch like fingers from a hand, and turn green to orange to red in a gradient from the top on down. I never liked tomatoes much before, but these ones are acidic and firm, and anyway, everything looks good to eat by lunchtime, when you're four water bottles deep and sweating tears that burn.

My sweat smells like ammonia now; the internet says I'm either dehydrated, need to eat more carbohydrates, or will suffer a fatal kidney rupture tomorrow. The carb thing is funny, because I'm so tired and stiff all the time that my diet is mostly dry toast.

We harvest the cherry tomatoes tenderly into big white buckets, leaving their small green hats on so that they will be less likely to split and weep juice in transport. At market, Boss said, people might be ready to cry over them.

This morning Kristy and I drove by a man dragging a deer carcass down the shoulder of the highway with his bare hands, pulling on its front feet as if trying to change its mind about entering a room. Yesterday the first living being I made eye contact with was a chicken walking down the road. Other than work, I've been staying home, sitting on my porch and trying to untangle these knots in silence.

All day we experience things.

Pena spoke up when I recounted the deer thing to Gwynn and said that the man was bringing the carcass to "The Roadkill Van." He sees one driving around the experimental turf fields on campus sometimes, piloted by a university intern majoring in wildlife management. It's not that big a deal, he said.

We tell each other good morning, good afternoon, and good evening as greetings. Only goodnight is always goodbye. This is the open-and-shut nature of our days, how the sun always sets and we always listen to it.

My left pinky finger has started popping out of its second joint again, the one closest to my hand, whenever I bend it. The feeling gives me a terrible fear on a primordial level. At the same time, I can't stop doing it, testing it. We spend hours crawling down the hoop house pathways picking big fat tomatoes and arranging them gently on flat trays; we need our hands for everything.

Gwynn told me to tape the pinky to its neighboring fingers. This makes me even more useless in the field. Everyone pretends they can't tell how far behind I am, but I feel them watching. The tape edges fill up with dirt. If it is going to help me heal, it has not yet. Still, like most things, I'll probably wake up one day to find the problem gone and forget I ever had it. That's another thing I like about physical pain—the way it disappears behind you.

Deer have been jumping over the electric fence meant to keep them out and eating the ivylike sweet potato vines off the ground, chewing them down to almost nothing. This afternoon, while the rest of us strung another level of twine around the field tomatoes, Gwynn and Boss constructed a fifteen-foot black cage of zip-tied bird netting over the yams. I said, Do you think that's high enough? like a joke, and Boss said, You wouldn't believe how these guys can fly.

Then he hocked a loogie onto the ground. He expects we can still save the crop, since the fruits are underground.

"The Cube," as we're calling it, struck me as this incredible art installation. Everything is so absurd, from the weird lunches we eat to the guy in line behind me at Wesco last week who said he was about to be arrested for insider trading at Colgate-Palmolive to the woman this morning running her kid along the shoulder of the highway on a backpack leash.

Perhaps I could be better, at the very least less enmeshed in futility, if I stopped observing, if I directed my eyes away from other people. Thinking about trying to go to church again to see whether anything really has changed, hoping for some kind of signal.

I can't bend my knees at all anymore. They just don't give. I went to urgent care secretly last month, where they told me nothing was wrong.

When we transplant, I have to be the one freeing the little seedlings from their trays and dropping them to the ground for everyone else to pull dirt around. It's lettuce and cauliflower and broccoli and kohlrabi and kale season. Everything smells of hot fertilizer and dry loam. It hasn't rained in four weeks. We try to balance our irrigation use between letting the plants die and running the well dry. Kristy tells me repeatedly to make sure the lettuce hits the ground facing upwards. Don't break those tiny tender leaves.

Before I began here, I believed that while working in the fields I would have time to pray. When things hurt, I thought, I'd offer them up. Turns out it's easier to be edified by your suffering when you have the energy to think about what it means and where it goes.

Offering it up used to be on my mind all the time. I don't know where I heard the idea; maybe in a folk song or on the radio sermons I listened to in my car when I felt especially spiritually isolated, loosed in a world whose reasoning I couldn't connect to and didn't know how to discuss. It sounds vaguely Protestant, the idea that we can remove pain from ourselves for somebody else to use. Also, that the suffering itself is a bad thing, by its nature waiting to be transformed into some other, higher purpose if we're good enough to start the process. What if it just happens, and the transformation is in us learning to take it?

I don't have problems with Protestants, by the way. We used to skip around all kinds of churches when I was young until my mother had her vision. Most of the time that doesn't weigh on my mind more than anything else; I just know it's there, the origin point of whatever my life might be about. I've talked about it with exactly one person before, a religious guy I really liked but also feared. He said that she was schizophrenic and I should probably be in jail myself for enabling her. Soon, one of us was probably going to kill the other, he said.

That might have something to do with why it was hard to answer Pena's question about whether I had prayed a novena for the healing of my knees. None of the words I know are enough to explain anything; if I don't try, it seems weak and ungrateful, but if I do, I get it wrong and cheapen the truth.

Gwynn was crawling ahead of us but turned her head back to listen, and Kristy stood at the edge of the field recording the planting in a dirty plastic binder not listening at all, and somewhere Boss was hitting the tractor pipe with a hammer again. *Please don't make me decide what to say,* was all I could think, *I don't know how.* I answered that no, I hadn't tried it.

Everybody is gracious about giving me the easy job—if I went to the doctor and they told me I should stop working, we would be, honestly, screwed—but I still feel a lot of guilt for everything that lives along the border of my ability to control it, like my body, and sometimes my mind.

I did try going to Mass again, and felt again like my heart was going to stop, or I was about to start snarling at my fellow parishioners for basically no reason. My knees are bad enough now that I can't kneel without searing pain. I've got get out of here. The churches are so big that they appear empty when half the pews are full.

I looked at my permanently dirty hands and wondered if anyone would understand how they'd gotten that way, would know that I did try to scrub them clean. I'm still listening, I insisted to whoever might have been listening to me.

Walking home alone through small old neighborhoods and over the bridge across the expressway, my calves spiraling into cramps, I felt strangely similar to the way I did after my second day of work at the farm, when everything seemed so eternally alive and functional that I went for a run.

Hell!

We have a whole hoop house of cucumbers at this point in the season, their thin spiky vines trellised up on the twine hooked onto the overhead cables just like the tomatoes. They make our hands itchy and their wide round leaves don't let much air through. Warped yellow fruit, stunted at the ends, hangs everywhere.

The vines are a few feet long and nearly dead. Some of them have blight, seemingly at random, and the hoop house is full of big brown diamond squash bugs eating the rest even though we put bug netting up to keep them out. Blight makes the fruit shrivel up and die, followed by the rest of the plant. Where the squash bugs haven't eaten the plants, they lay clutches of tiny copper eggs which we have to rip from the leaves and crush.

The landscape fabric—stapled to the dirt around the plants to keep the weeds down—is reusable and surrounded the chard last year. Chard and cucumber suffer common diseases, which Kristy said is probably the cause of all this, the blight and the eggs surviving the winter. The sides of the hoop house are rolled closed, so no airborne spores will travel, and it was so hot you couldn't believe.

None of us could see any way the cucumber plants would survive, even Gwynn and I who don't know anything, but Boss still had us clip the newest lengths of the vines higher up on the twine. We clean our hands with bleach coming in and out of the hoop house to avoid transferring disease. I asked Kristy if it was bad for you to eat the fruit of a blighted plant and she yelled at me about how much worse every other mode of production on earth is for human health.

Whenever I look upward, I feel dizzy and lost.

We all went completely silly in the heat, and were so surprised by our good moods that we got even happier. Pena, who is most of the time separate, said very seriously, You guys are in the goofy dome today. We agreed we could have laid down on the ground and laughed for an hour.

Instead, we killed squash bugs with our slick fingers.

Kristy told Boss that the crew had a hard time with this in past seasons—the killing act, I mean—and it didn't save the cucumbers last year, so maybe we shouldn't do it.

He shrugged and said, You have to do things you don't like in life.

Then he wandered away. It's amazing how good he is at disappearing, even on this very open land. I talk to myself like he talks to us. Every day I expect to finally prevail over my instincts to maintain my own comfort.

The smell the bugs let out when you crush them—I just can't tell you.

Shane's on vacation and lent me his car while he's gone so I can get a break from carpooling with Kristy. On the last ten minutes of my drive to work today, I hit and obliterated a small bird. I thought it would move. I always stop for them and they always move.

It happened right on the way into the village next to the farm, at the four-way stop. The sun was just about coming up and I had the windows open to feel the air. I had really just been thinking how wonderful it was to be alive and to see things, even the difficult parts, all of it together.

Another car sat at the opposing stop sign with its turn signal on, so I waited there, but the man behind the wheel stared straight ahead, perfectly still. I waited and his face didn't even twitch. I drove the rest of the way fast. When I got to the farm, I looked all over the car but couldn't even find a feather. It made me feel good that I didn't cry. See, I'm tough. I don't care about squash bugs and I don't care about this.

I'm tired of sick and evil things happening.

The fog was heavy this morning, too, not just on the rivers and the low places in the fields, but all over the ground. It only appeared once I got out of the city, which I was glad for. When the fog comes into town and makes everything pink and I have to see a P.F. Chang's sign shining through it like a beacon, I feel that I could just roll over and die. For some reason I think I'm not supposed to say this, but I am beginning to hate the sights of human activity.

While scrubbing salad muck from our harvest buckets today, Gwynn wanted to know what I thought about the inherent selfishness of striving for eternal salvation. I imagined putting my head in the industrial salad spinner drum and drowning myself with centrifugal force. Then I wished I were a more generous person.

I also wish that I could talk to her about what I think. Everything beyond the material realities of my life is a closed circuit I contain and spend my life inside, but there is no connection between this world and the external one, no off-ramp connecting me to whoever I'm looking at.

I couldn't tell her I don't worry about that question because my concern with goodness is not for want of reward but for the sake of doing what I ought to have done, that actually I don't think the pursuit of salvation is selfish at all if it's one you're making honestly.

I said we might as well try for the good if someone tells us it is there. It hadn't occurred to me until then that we often repeat the same conversation. She finished scrubbing the last bucket and I walked to the other side of the table to start hosing the soap bubbles off so she could follow with the disinfectant pressure sprayer.

We have been doing this exact task for months and I still often miscalculate and tip the buckets off the table at an angle that fills my knee boots up with cold water.

The music act at market today was a punk rock cover band in their forties. Gwynn went home early because she felt sick from the heat the day before and Ryan was sleeping in his van up north all weekend and although I never stopped moving for the customers, it felt like no one was really there all day.

I kept spacing out while packing up because I was thinking about the big old-timey airplane that we see loop-de-looping over the fields sometimes, and about how Kristy hates it, the idea of some old man thinking he's delighting us—she thinks he thinks that—and about how she prefers it when the vultures circle overhead because it's more honest.

The cover band singer came over to ask if I needed help, which his male bandmates loudly chastised him for. She knows what she's doing, man! She does this all the time! And I could have used some help, really, but felt embarrassed to accept it after that.

About a hundred degrees again today, weeding between the Brussels sprouts and broccoli heads and cauliflower stems, which right now are just spindly trees of red and purple about six inches high, shedding leaves under the sun. Because they are all in the cruciferous family, you can barely the difference between them at this age. "Cruciferous" means "cross-bearing"—I learned that from the scientific name of a frog we often saw when I worked at the nature center—but I don't know how it relates to the plants. Anyhow, we planted almost an acre of them on the fresh-tilled back plots closest to the trees.

We weeded using the standing hoes with handles taller than us, which cast long shadows on the ground. It felt like a desert before a shootout.

Boss's mom, who works in the greenhouse starting seeds without pay three days a week, felt sorry for us and brought out popsicles from the barn freezer, which we ate one-handed while continuing to hoe because we aren't allowed to waste time. You can't lie about what you've done in the visible world.

Gwynn remembered I don't like the grape flavor and took that one to let Pena and I have the oranges. Kristy was off splicing cracked irrigation lines, so Boss's mom opened the fourth and bit it.

Take a break! she said, her mouth green.

No! we said.

We are in the doldrums, Pena said after she left and we

had dropped the popsicle sticks into the beds to compost. Gwynn asked what that meant, and he told us it was well-known in the farming community as the feeling you have when the fields and the months look endless and dead. The felt square of his scapular was stuck to his neck again but either he didn't notice or he wanted it there.

It's been six weeks since he invited me to play badminton. I turned down the invitation because of my pinky finger problem, and he hasn't asked me again.

Also, he said that he never listens to music and, like me, will sometimes just stare at the wall or window doing nothing but looking, thinking, for an hour or two. I wonder how similar our spiritual experiences are; we share all of it, on the surface, but don't seem to actually connect over that fact in any deep way.

Though we have almost nothing to say to each other, he's one of the few people I've met that I fundamentally respect, how he is so calm and remains himself around everybody else. I have been trying to be that way for as long as I can remember.

On the other hand, he told me that the idea of romance actually disgusts him, makes him sick, that love is gross and he yells at his parents to stop it when they hold hands around him. He's not down in the dirt with everybody else like I am and he never wants to be. I feel embarrassed to be entangled in this human mess in front of him, even though most of what I would measure as a success for my own life involves other people. He said today that his mother has started to sew him a new collection of canvas shorts now that he's almost five feet tall.

Stopped by the bakery down the road from the farm to buy more of those peanut butter seed balls, which are stupidly priced for something I could also eat from a bird feeder, but I think about them basically all day. It was my last chance to get one because tomorrow I have to return Shane's car. Kristy is thinner and tougher than I am, so I'd never ask her to stop for food.

A new teenager is working the register at the small store every time I come in. The baby-faced boy who helped me today asked where I was from.

When I told him he looked at me with these shiny eyes and said, awed, The City?

And I thought, this has to be a movie, but I'm just right here.

After that, sitting in the car facing the dumpster and eating the seed ball with the door open while the birds sang, I thought a few other things. When I was his age and we lived in the desert for a few years, my only future goal was to live somewhere with sidewalks. I wrote that in my diary with a check box next to it followed by *learn to roller skate.*

Having lived in cities now for less than ten years, it feels as if I never came from anywhere else, that I can't undo it, and for some reason I desperately want to, to sort of unwind the so-called civilization out of myself, and the way all that noise manifests itself in a person when you talk to them, how you can see it on their faces when they don't live in a physical reality beyond their own functions, but I guess this kid probably would just like to have more friends nearby to hang out with.

He came out the side door and down the little ramp carrying the last slice of thin pizza from the heat lamp rotisserie next to the register, the paper plate covered in a sheen of cold orange oil, and said he would have to throw it away if I didn't want it. The bakery would be closing for the day soon. I wished he couldn't see my sweaters and coffee mugs all over Shane's car and the dirt on my swollen knees, although he was sweaty himself and smelled of old grease.

His shirt, which was hidden by his apron before, read I PAUSED MY GAME FOR THIS? over a drawing of a video game controller. I took the pizza from him and said thank you more times than I needed to.

I've managed to avoid eggplant harvests since they started four weeks ago, but today Kristy was trying to fix something on the tractor (Boss still hasn't taught her to drive it, but she is responsible for maintaining it) so I had to. The eggplants grow hidden under the leaves of terribly spiky plants that always make us sneeze. They grow up to our thighs and the eggs hang down from drooping stalks, white until they ripen. The stalks are so hard they require special clippers. We don't wear gloves most of the time for some reason, but we always do in there.

Eggplants give market customers more anxiety than anything else we sell. I never have the energy to prepare them myself—I've eaten toast for dinner for the last six days—so I parrot back the suggestions of other vendors. If you salt them first, the bitterness goes out. I love to puree them and make baba ganoush.

Gwynn tells me she's amazed by how easy it is for me to make up these answers. I think it is probably a glaring character flaw, but it sells a lot of eggplant.

Onion harvest today. It was a hundred degrees by sunrise, and their tops had grown so dense with weeds that the onions held the heat of the full sun and let humidity loose on our faces as we plunged into their bed. The days have been so long and so humid and so frantic that I've almost stopped thinking about my personal life. I miss my parents and the ocean; I feel as if I'll spend the rest of my life here instead. Any choices I could make are far away now.

We spent two days weeding twenty-two beds in May and another two in June, then let them go, and some of the weeds grew taller than us. The onions were easy to pull up, though, ten beds of white ones with golden skin pushing above the ground and six of red plus two each of two shallot varieties.

We yanked six or seven at a time by their green wet tubular tops, then laid them out one layer deep in plastic bread trays. It felt artful arranging the bulbs like that, but it had to be done fast, without precision. Thin layers of onion skins drifted in the muggy air behind us. The bread trays were flat black plastic with higher walls and DELIGHT BAKERIES THEFT PROSECUTED printed in white on all four sides.

Boss had us leave the trays behind on the ground once we filled them, then walk back to pick them up and carry them to the waiting wagon bed attached to the sputtering tractor. Each is about thirty pounds when full.

Kristy counted how many times we raised the trays and set them down using this method (five to six times, variable, a twofold multiplier of unnecessary labor). It is exciting when she takes us into her confidence and complains aloud; we all brighten up a little when she does. She asked to harvest right onto the wagon and drive it into the greenhouse so as to minimize our movements, using the success of the row cover rollers as an example of her good judgment, but Boss said no and reminded us that having a good attitude is the key to a functional workplace.

She wants this farm to be better and all of us to be better, so much so that it seems to be driving her truly insane. I almost admire how deeply she is able to care about things that are not hers and people who do not listen to her.

Around row five, Kristy began talking about the inefficient harvest style of past years, when Boss' ex-wife would "just be crawling around." Bugs flew up from the humid tangled plants, buzzing around our ears and the sweat in our hair. She told me I wasn't pulling enough onion tops with each hand and that I wasn't thinking about my motions when delivering them to the bread tray. I'm sure she was right.

Carpooling has been making me feel really bad about myself, although I wish it didn't matter, wish I was not trying so hard to minimize my psychic presence in her Subaru. I'm sure she can feel that I care and recoils further in response. She turns public radio on when she picks me up before daybreak and leaves it on until she drops me off in the evening. This week she started putting a towel on my seat like you would do for a dog and I wanted to scream at her. Instead I said nothing, not trusting myself to talk.

Pena worked silently, yards ahead of us, a perfect machine.

Everyone always talks about wise movements. I wonder what those are and how to learn them.

By four o'clock, fifty bread trays full of onions were stacked four or five high on the wagon bed. Our shirts stuck to us and our eyes hurt. Boss drove the wagon next to the greenhouse, where we lifted and carried and rearranged them one layer deep across a low shaky table. We'll do the reverse in a few weeks when the onion tops have dried out and the bulbs are ready to store inside the cooler over winter.

The table was made of grid wire balanced on overturned buckets across the length of the greenhouse. It was even hotter inside and none of us spoke at all, except for Gwynn, who wanted to try singing work songs, something she learned on Instagram.

It's the twenty-first century, Pena said to her dismissively while receiving a tray from off the wagon, which felt like watching a kindergartener shoot a rifle. Kristy was shuffling across the grid wire with the full trays, the end of the line, and started laughing. She lost her balance and her leg went through one of the table's wire squares.

Afterwards, we posed in the greenhouse doorway for a picture to put in the newsletter that Boss' mom sends out. The sides of the building are rimmed with tall stinging nettles and we had to crowd near each other to avoid getting burned.

Gwynn said in my ear that it was a human rights violation for us to work in this weather. The cloudy plastic thermometer wired to the greenhouse's wooden door panel read 106. Pena wrung sweat out of his brown felt scapular. When I looked down at my thighs afterward, waiting at the picnic table for Kristy to get some seconds tomatoes from the cooler, the skin seemed to be moving in a vortex towards the point where my eyes were focused. You can't spend too much time in the cooler right out of the sun or you'll make yourself sick.

On the drive home I wanted to ask her to pull over because I felt like I was about to black out, but I didn't. I clutched the fennel head I brought with me, tracing its branching layers and knowing I probably wouldn't cook it. Since the camping ordeal I have been practicing my control over myself and clenching my stomach muscles. Anne finally texted, upset that I didn't seem to have had fun on the trip. She said she would have written sooner but wanted to wait until she wasn't angry at me anymore. Maybe this is it between us.

I don't know why I don't feel more about it. At night I manage to tell God that I still want guidance and don't know what to do, and in the morning I manage to give thanks for another day, but other than that I just get up and then go to bed.

Kristy turned down the radio about halfway back to the city because she was tired of hearing about the president and talked about her plans to go to the gym and then make gallons of salsa that evening. Wow, I said, and really meant it. Her limbs look wiry, like the idea of a farmer you get when you hear the word, and nothing seems to hurt her.

I admire everyone else's tolerance for everything.

Boss is sending Gwynn to work the other Saturday market on the east side with his mother, so he and I have the city stall now. Gwynn can't afford the gas money on Saturdays when she isn't getting paid for eight hours and the eastern market is closer to her house. She said Boss told her sternly that she should have considered her financial circumstances before taking this job. Pena and I gave her all the cash we had on Friday so she could buy gas to get home and she looked angry at us.

Boss is picking me up for market now because I haven't made any progress on buying a car. I tell him I'm looking, but the truth is I'm not looking very hard. Something is going to happen to me soon, I think, and I don't yet know what type of vehicle it will require.

I waited on the steps for him this morning and got nervous, a first day of school anxiety. The changes to the schedule reminded me that this season is going to end and things will have to be different again (and again and again!). I keep trying to remember this when I'm exhausted or miserable—how much I'll miss it one day, how it'll look so much better when it becomes a memory.

Boss turned down his riot grrrl music to ask me how I was when I got in the van, and I said I'm okay, how are you? and he actually pulled over to ask what was wrong that I was only okay, not good. Those words are interchangeable to me, which is what I told him, and he said gravely that their implications are much different.

Kristy has noted his inability to acknowledge any negative realities, but it seems like he's not ignoring anything, like he actually believes it all must be good. When he swung the van back onto the street, the movement toppled a tomato tray in the back, and we heard them rolling all the way up the hill. Well, that's not good, he said, turning the music up again.

First melon harvest today. Three colors of watermelon, four types of cantaloupes. The vines have all died back—they covered the field totally, close to two feet high, for months—and now we walk through without getting scratched by anything, picking up the ripe fruits. My knees are slightly less pained now that we harvest more than we plant and weed, which means less crawling and squatting.

We stack the melons inside tall orange crates and haul them back to the golf cart, where Gwynn drives them back up to the barn to sit in the cooler. They're heavy but fun to hold; there's something sporting about their shape that makes you want to throw them.

We'll make a few passes through as the stragglers catch up to their siblings. The watermelons you test by their color and shape, the cantaloupes by whether their beige skins have an orange undertone. When the watermelons are all rounded out and develop a little green patch on the bottom, you can eat them; when the cantaloupes aren't green but aren't too confident of an orange, you can pick them up.

These clues don't matter that much because they also just fall right off the vine when they're ready, loose in your hand.

Overripe cantaloupes have little thumbprints of orange shining where the flesh has rotted through the beige rind. We throw them underhand out of the field and they explode into the pathways. The riper they are, the more readily they burst and the further out the seeds spray. Pena and I had a pitching contest (he beat me for distance on every toss) until Kristy told us to stop.

We shared yellow watermelons at lunch, cutting them in halves and eating them with spoons. Kristy said she always eats the little white and brown seeds. *Her* digestive system can handle them. I could tell you what she's eaten for dinner every night for the last five months. Dinner is the safest thing to talk about.

Kristy seems to detect and to hate some cowardice or related inefficiency in all of us; when she points it out, I want to agree, though I don't know what exactly it is, or how to root it out of myself.

Anne came over on Sunday and we walked to the bakery around the corner and bought croissants and ate them on the floor of my living room like we used to do. I invited her in a crazed, last-ditch effort to make things normal. With the hot weather and my focus on work and my possible conversion of heart, I'd been feeling more malleable, and kinder maybe, and I thought I could either salvage something between us or create a smooth off-ramp in the event there was nothing left to salvage.

She called me pretentious when she saw the book on the coffee table about the history of American architectural styles. She often makes these comments about the music I like and the clothes I wear and the way I talk and even my going to the farm. I see what she means and am harsh with myself about it too, but I really am reading the book. When I mentioned that Shane told me one of our old professors had tried to become a professional wrestler while on sabbatical, Anne went silent and short, asking when I'd had time to see him.

She still seemed angry about the camping trip, too, which felt a little unfair because I was the one whose car exploded from the effort of maintaining our friendship. When I asked her, she said I didn't seem to care about her. I told her I did but I just didn't have the energy to be around in the same way anymore. She said she didn't believe that, and I said if she didn't want to understand me, I didn't know what to tell her. We made Bloody Marys in my kitchen and after that it was easy to talk about people we used to see around campus and things we remembered.

This was another new town, where I made new friends again, and where again it turned out we shared little beyond being in the same place at the same time. I'm not sure whether people can change, whether I'm too idealistic to be so convinced that we can, that we always are. Sometimes I sit in bed at night listening to my neighbors get drunk and fight and I cry about how alone I feel. I've never really belonged somewhere socially, made sense to somebody other than Red.

So what? Who doesn't feel that way? Pena doesn't like his classmates, Kristy doesn't like us, the work still has to get done.

When Anne got up from the living room rug for a glass of water, I raised my eyes to the ceiling like those statues in church again and thought *God, please help me, please use this for something,* and the sound of the faucet laboring to run and Sarah from Facebook's romcom playing through her door was almost something I could bear.

When Anne's boyfriend came to take her back to the east side of the state, where she just moved in with him to be close to his graduate program in business administration, I stood in the doorway and almost convinced myself we would never see each other again. I'd wrestled so long with my duty to never give up that the thought there was nothing I could do made me feel almost frighteningly free.

I closed myself in the bathroom and looked at my face in the cheap, age-spotted mirror and stretched the curls out of my hair with my fingers. After that I brushed my teeth for a long while and spat my mouthwash into the sink about seven times, staring down at the green foam on the silver top of the drain.

Then it was like I had no thoughts or feelings at all, standing there. If only the same thing could happen at work. There, though, I live the kind of life you can't detach from.

It finally rained in the middle of the night, nearly drowning the newly seeded lettuce and salad. Other farms flooded and lost entire crops. When we arrived the next morning, the humidity was hard to talk through. Our legs started to sweat, our ankles and wrists and ears, before we even made it to the beet field.

Boss said he was glad he'd invested in getting drainage tiles installed under the field pathways before he had to make alimony payments.

This earth appears so solid that it's hard to picture just picking it up and putting some plastic underneath. The tomatoes out in the field absorbed so much overdue water that they turned grainy and soft. We thought they were diseased and weren't sure whether to harvest them.

We have so much at market now that it doesn't fit the table and we stack it all on top of itself, the lettuce and scallions and peppers and eggplants and onions and melons and most of the beans, on overturned crates and bins several layers deep. I can hardly reach over them to pick up carrots for people.

I like how I just keep moving the whole time, how I can't think about anything. Trying to imagine an entire life this way. Maybe I'm getting better at ceding control to something beyond myself, at looking and listening to what's actually happening, even though I don't realize it day to day.

Either way, it's really clear now that I love working because it takes up all the empty space, even as I regret that all I do is work or recover from working, recovery which stops me from filling up the empty space.

Every farmer I know loves to live the hard way, but we don't really talk about it. You're not just supposed to do the work; you're supposed to bear the pain of it gracefully, or perhaps love the pain, get something out of it. This week, Gwynn talked a lot about how expensive it's getting to drive to work in her fuel-inefficient car, and Kristy yelled at her for half an hour about how you cannot quit and you *must see this through* because *you committed.* Aside from the social world, I have bought into this idea without realizing it, and I'm still not sure if I actually have more physical issues than the rest of them to make it more difficult or if my character is just weaker.

Maybe in part the suffering is proving something, that you can withstand it all, that you have transcended the needs of the flesh and can press on towards a completion you won't reach. The farm never ends.

Nobody appears spiritual about this or the work of their lives, though, not even those who are religious, like Pena. You do it, and that's it. People I know with desk jobs or post-grad internships they complete from their living rooms seem to have much more urgent spiritual questions. To my family members, the career sufferers I know best, every problem you have is something you can solve, no matter how long you've wrestled with it.

Maybe the work fills up all the space made for asking what you're doing or why you're doing it or who you are or how you got there or where you are going, standing room only for the spirit. Still, I have to imagine that something beyond the self must be present to compel a person to feel pain willingly in this day and age.

I remember talking to Red earlier in the season and thinking that there was no such thing as harmony with nature like people say, because it's never been an independently living thing to me, but a force to respond to. Maybe engaging in the struggle in first place, having something visible to push against, is part of what I mean.

The most exquisite suffering comes when working with the field tomatoes. Every part of growing them tests you.

We can only pick in the afternoon because if you touch them when they're wet with dew, disease spreads through the water. The rows are surrounded by black landscape fabric, so the sun is drawn right to you when you stand on it. Now the vines have grown into dense, almost impenetrable cubes between the strings holding them upright; rooting around in there to harvest feels like hunting for catfish by plunging your hands into mudholes on the riverbank.

Every week we have to string another round of plastic rope between the T-posts to hold up the new growth, which is heavy and floppy and snarled and itchy, and the tension of the plastic rope burns our hands. This twine is supposed to biodegrade in the sun, someday, the packaging says.

The tomatoes that go bad between harvest days fall to the fabric and turn into a rotting stew to crawl through. It collects in the dips of the landscape fabric and smells like a dying sun.

Anyway, I don't mean to complain, and I shouldn't, or don't want to, really, it's just that I feel like my life is something I'm always enduring, waiting for each task or day or season to end, and no matter how I talk to myself I can't talk myself into a place where I enjoy things, even though on the intellectual level I do enjoy everything, and am so grateful for my life.

We arrange the tomatoes one layer deep on flat gray trays which lock into each other on the corners when stacked. The larger tomatoes go on the sides of the trays and the smaller ones in the middle, where the weight of the trays above causes the plastic to bulge and crush any fruits that rise to touch it. Gwynn likes riding on the back of the golf cart to hold the swaying towers still on the way back up to the wash barn. There, we weigh them and shuffle them into the cooler on carts with wheels that don't want to turn.

Boss's mother suggested we take the unsellable tomatoes home, peel them, slice them into segments, and freeze them in plastic bags for easy sauce-making come wintertime. What a clean little world to live in.

I was thinking last night about how I can't quite get to the bottom of anything in my mind lately, wondering if I have some kind of illness, but then I realized I'm just not thinking very much at all, for once; it's empty in there. The sun bleached it out.

After work I sat on the couch trying to read my pretentious architecture book, and getting up the energy to walk ten steps and go to bed took half an hour. It isn't really a couch but a pair of matching loveseats that Nate had borrowed his dad's truck to help me move from the apartment of a Facebook stranger two years ago. At the time, I couldn't believe I had friends who would spend their weekends helping me with such boring tasks. It didn't seem possible that things would go sour between people like us, would ever get worse.

Harvested cantaloupes again today. Third pass through the field. Most of them are rotten by now, soft and creamsicle orange in patches where they lie on the ground. They smell like sickness and sugar. When I pick them up to pitch them, my thumbs break right through the weak skin. I think I could do the same to my own brain sometimes.

Something about the truth dampens my ability to muster it.

Thinking again about how long it's been since I heard from Red and wanting to tell him things I'm not sure I even believe. Finally having let go of Anne, or at least coming to terms with the idea, makes me miss him more. I know things will be different soon, but it's hard to hold hope in the meantime. Confessing just to feel something doesn't mean much, does it?

Boss and Kristy and I stayed late into the evening harvesting green beans on our knees. One of the six rows of beans is actually purple and another white, but the larger category of bean is "green." This is probably the last harvest before we let the plants go, then till them under.

I love beans because you sit down when you harvest them. The wide bushy leaves grow to your kneecaps, and you collect pods by kneeling and pushing the plants around in a slow circle: back, to the left, towards you, and to the right, pulling pods and dropping them into white five-gallon buckets. There's just something so silly about the whole thing, the words and the shapes.

Everybody else hates the process because it is so time-consuming—four rows take six hours—and Boss allows us overtime for this crop only. On Friday, Pena and Gwynn went home, but Kristy and I wanted to stay. After a while Boss let Kristy go harvest the lettuce we didn't get to earlier while he and I finished the beans. She can't relax unless we make it through the harvest checklist.

It was a little cooler by then, and breezy, and the cars went by on the highway and the little birds fought and the leaves rustled. My knees felt good where they were bent under me. Boss just kept talking and talking, like he does whenever he works with us, but it was easy this time because I could tell he just liked to be hearing something.

He told all kinds of bar stories and things he and his ex-wife used to do when he was young and 'silly.' One time, he got lost in New Orleans for two entire days. I probably said too much about my life in return but told myself it didn't matter. Someday we'll all be dust in the wind. Kristy and I ate a whole bunch of soft raw beans in the car on our way home, and even then, the sun wouldn't set for another two hours.

While harvesting kale alone at sunrise, I felt happier than I ever had in my life.

It came out of nowhere, pushing up to my sternum; I wasn't afraid of it leaving, but I wondered what would make it go. I stood there watching the pink sky rip itself into orange, my legs already wet with cold dew, and observed the feeling.

I rarely experience active *happiness* or any other extreme, just this general level of being that drifts in one direction or the other. No switch has flipped. Still, there are two worlds now, the one I live in and the one I think about. Maybe the first one is getting stronger.

Gwynn joined me in the field late with a rusty harvest cart bumping behind her; her car had been about to overheat, so she had to stop for a while on her drive in.

I feel happier than I ever have in my life right now, I said, to see if it would go away. She counted kale leaves across from me slowly and deliberately, sliding them from one hand to the other like cards in a deck.

Yay! she said, looking up and smiling widely.

I have these rubber bands stretched across my hands and I pick the dew-wet kale with my fingers. I never seem to get any faster. I'll be glad when it's over. I always drop what

I need to hold onto and then I pick it up again. I can do it, I can do it, I can do it.

Should be in school again now, I suppose, but I don't feel strange about it. Everyone off the farm asks me if I do. Don't you miss it? Don't you feel so lost? No.

Getting cold in the mornings. The summer peaked and disappeared. I put my sweaters on, I take my sweaters off, I see the school buses coming and going on the state road that borders the fields. I'd never realized before how the air changes hour by hour.

Cabbage harvests this week. For the Napa, which are about a foot tall and crunchy like Styrofoam, you test readiness by pushing down on the top. If the head feels firm, you can saw them from the thin stem where they stand upright. They are all full of worms, and we have to peel inches of leaves away before reaching a core that's clean from the slimy tunnels chewed through them.

I'm not allegorical! I'm never signifying anything!

The other cabbages—the regular cabbage, the Dutch flat, and the cone-shaped ones that Gwynn named Sweethearts at market (we lay them out in the trays to form two halves of a heart)—are heavy and solid, things that could concuss you. We cut them when they look big enough, which you're just supposed to have a sense for.

Kristy said the insect poop didn't bother her. She said this proudly, with her chin sticking out, because I made a face when some of it flew into my hair.

I find myself watching everything I say even more than before, especially now that it's too cold to feel my hands when I come inside. Although I am not personally invested in my coworkers, this feeling reminds me of Red and Anne and everyone who came before them—metering myself appropriately to be as inoffensive as possible.

Sick of it. Trying to pray and to mean it, but can't focus.

Am I bothering you? I actually asked Kristy last week when she made a backhanded comment in the beet field. Every time I try to speak to her sincerely, she acts like she has no idea what I'm talking about—I thought it embarrassed her, so I stopped until I lost my temper—but this time she said No, and then five minutes later said, Sorry I'm such an asshole, I'm just being mean for no reason, which actually made me feel a lot worse.

Pena had stopped working behind us to look at the shriveled bok choy inside the groundhog trap that's been lying in the aisle for weeks. It looked like he wanted to put his hand in there. I kind of did too. There's just something about an unsprung spring.

The trap hasn't caught anything. Boss said he sits on his porch with a shotgun after work every night, watching, waiting, drinking beer. That was what made him a country person, he said, when he first spent an evening outside waiting to kill something.

The cornfields we pass in the mornings get shaved down a bit more each day. The stalks look colorless now and the tree lines end sharply against them. Usually, the harvesters are left out overnight to pick up right where they left off. I can't believe the size of some of the tractors, or that we do the same work, these machines and the rest of us.

While weeding between the rutabagas, Pena reenacted a fight at his family's homeowners association over the right of the individual to put heavy chemicals down on their yards. The decorative pond at the center of the development has become a dead zone from all the runoff, toads floating dead in the blue water, but people want to keep their grass bright, he said.

He knows a lot about grass, seemingly against his will—he mows lawns on the weekends and tells us sometimes about his classmates in the state college horticulture department majoring in grass management, whom he calls "turf bros." It's funny to hear a word like "bro" coming from such an agelessly somber face.

They will grow up to manage golf courses and baseball fields; they love a sheet of flat green grass like nothing else, and he says most of them spit dip.

Right now, on the other side of the state, they are lamenting that "turf season" is almost at an end. Pena told us this while focusing on tearing a slice of white bread into very small pieces at the picnic table under the big maple tree. He had rutabaga mud all over his face. I love the way he talks about people, like a scientist describing fish in an aquarium with one arm twisted behind his back, but my absolute favorite thing about him is that he doesn't like the taste of vegetables.

The weather has turned grey and I feel some kind of violent sadness with nothing real behind it. Every year, wherever I am, it is so easy to lean backwards into this autumn gloom. Still, something warm and living makes itself known at random moments now, pushing on my lungs from the inside. The greatest act of faith is being hopeful, my mother said.

Kristy took her five days of vacation this week so Boss lent me his old beater car to get to and from work. She didn't tell us where she went, said something vague about plans with her brother. (What brother? How does she manage to work here and reveal so little about herself?) The car is a sedan the color of a sugar snap pea that scrapes along the ground and has carpeted seats. I forgot that hot dust smell, the way the cars all smelled when I was younger.

It's nice to drive around in; it's nice to drive at all. Funny also how the car itself makes me feel like someone different, like the type of person who would have an old pea-green sedan, whatever that means. There are so many people to be and so many of them take shape around the boundaries of physical things, this car or that haircut.

Yesterday I went to the Salvation Army store on the west side strip mall road with the staff who are always talking about the parties they've been to and the bitches they see there. I've missed the freedom to go places, but might have been better off without the distraction. I was covered in potato harvest dirt and left without touching anything because I felt so out of place. When I bent my cracking knees, sprinkles of fine dirt fell free to the linoleum.

It rained so hard on my way home that I couldn't see through the old windshield even with the wipers scraping on their most frantic setting, and I got so nervous I could hardly breathe thinking I'd die right there from an obscured oncoming car before I discerned how to put my life to any good use. I had to pull into the small parking lot of a Burrito Boy to calm down. I tried to wait out the rain there but it just kept coming, and the parking lot was crowded with people and the Styrofoam soda cups they dropped when they were done with them.

Today I stopped at a liquor store halfway home and bought a few tall beers. Two women were working there, one of them smoking inside, talking back and forth about a junior league soccer game. I got this really sudden, crushing desire to be as wholly part of a life as they were. Then I told myself to quit being such a sad sack already.

The smoking one called me sweetie and told me to have a good night. I felt strange and pathetic walking out of there with the brown paper bag.

Still didn't want to end my traveling and sit down and look at myself, so stopped by the river park about halfway home and stood on the bank of a stream for a while. I felt like I should have changed my life already, standing there, like I was a year behind or maybe twenty and still too afraid to catch up, and I cried for a length of time that embarrassed me even though no one was watching. I could hear the highway but couldn't see it, knew the suburban developments were there but couldn't see them either. It was nice to know no one was able to look at me for once.

Said some scattered prayers and got a real kind of physical fear inside about nothing in particular. *Whatever it is I should do*, I thought, *I'll do it, and I'm sorry.* I remembered one time in college when I was sitting in the woods outside my dorm at night and felt completely convinced someone was standing right behind me breathing into my hair.

I always feel better driving around after I've cried. It turns me into a serious presence behind the wheel.

When I got home from the park, I ate some soup from a box and went to bed without drinking either beer.

Sometimes after I've been standing at our market stall for a few hours while people walk by, they start to break apart from their humanity and I'm just watching puppets on parade. If I see too much, I can't locate the soul anymore. Everyone is just arms, heads, funny-looking jeans. This experience is peaceful. It's a relief to depart from the world in any small way.

We harvested all the squash this week and laid it in the field to cure. The outside layer of the green and orange and yellow and pink skins will set in the sun for the next seven days, turning them hard and long-lasting. Boss has had one sitting on his kitchen counter for three years and it's still perfectly good, still smiles with the face his ex-wife drew on it in ballpoint pen before they divorced.

In previous years, squash dried in the greenhouse instead, but it is still full of onions because we are behind schedule. Kristy was deeply distressed by the new plan, certain a rain would come and rot everything to mush, although it has not yet. No one seems to hear her speak much these days. I try harder to listen but this irritates her more, which I guess I understand. My earnestness frustrates me, too.

Cut the spinning-top acorn squash from their vines and the long pink Candyroasters, two feet long with green tips at the pointed ends, the little decorative pumpkins with names like Autumn Frost, the huge warty squashes with thick green alligator skin. I will never eat any of them—squash makes me feel rotten. Its aftertaste leaves me not quite right.

The vines have shriveled up and died on the dry ground below them, so most of our work was done. Just had to make the final separation.

I left Boss's car at the farm and rode home with Kristy. Told him I would be interested in buying it (he wants an "eligible bachelor upgrade"), and he told me he'd think about it. I feel very lonely and trapped by all this nothingness around me, this air cushion. I have to change my life, I know. Who would I be with a car? Anybody different? Same old me, leaning against it at night in the overgrown lot out behind my apartment, looking up, waiting?

Working outside has kept me from other harms, and maybe that should be enough, at least enough for gratitude.

Disassembled the netting cage, or "The Cube," around the sweet potatoes so we could harvest them. I came in late with Shane's car because I had to get a tooth filled in the morning. I scheduled another appointment to fill another tooth that doesn't really need it yet in preparation for moving and having no dentist for a while, though I don't know for sure that either will happen. Passed the old church on the expressway driving in and knew I'd have to try it again. For today, I demonstrate my faith through the maintenance of my molars.

Forgot how in the autumn it looks like sunset all day. Boss tilled way deep in with the tractor and we scrabbled through the hard-compacted soil. Everything went pink in the angle of the light. Couldn't feel my face until well after lunchtime.

Sweet potatoes grow in blobs connected to each other from the base by ropy tubes the width of a pinky finger, like organs and veins. The idea is to trace the veins through the ground while digging to find the kidney-shaped tubers, but the surface is so hard that we must have missed plenty. The weight of the tractor compresses it down even more. We filled big orange plastic tubs and loaded them on the tractor forks for Boss to stack in the storage cooler.

While trying to put the bucket attachment back on the front of the tractor, later, he ended up bending the arm by ramming too hard at the wrong angle and had to beat it furiously with a hammer to straighten it back out.

Cracked a fingernail on the dirt. It hurt but I don't notice much anymore. Soil is jammed under all of my fingernails. Sometimes now I can just squint and wait and then things don't bother me. This much, at least, makes me feel like I'm succeeding in the way I interact with my reality.

As we clawed at the unforgiving ground, Gwynn told me about a trip she and her boyfriend took over the weekend to a submarine that had been turned into a museum. She thought about being dead when she was inside it and decided once and for all there really wasn't an afterlife. Her faith seems to depend on the question of heaven existing, so in effect the door has closed.

I have to tell myself she could change her mind again, even if that is an attempt to justify not taking the risk of trying to convince her. Then I wonder if I've failed her by being unable to talk more openly, and then I suppose that's presumptuous since it's her choice to make anyway, and so on in circles.

It's hard to understand being so affected by single moments, like standing in a metal tube at the side of the road by a cornfield with a man on a Saturday could actually change the rest of a life, spiritually speaking. I guess something similar happened when my car exploded (containers of movement!), but that was an event rather than a silence.

I've always had this sort of animal instinct about what God wants of me, something unnamed nudging me toward one action or another. The troubles I have are with how I live up to that internal direction more than a question of whether it's real. Without this in common, and no way to explain why I have it, I don't know how to say anything to her.

Moved irrigation lines around later from the cabbage to the beets, and packaged salad greens after lunch. Kristy and I listened to a musical variety hour on the drive home. She gave me the first compliment I have heard from her, which is that if I am familiar with the band CAN at the age of twenty-two, I am probably in good shape moving forward.

I thought, but didn't say, that I really owe her one, because I bought the foam clogs she wears and recommended to me last month, and now my knees hurt a lot less, and my calves and my ankles too, things I didn't even realize weren't right. There's all this vacant space where the pain used to be and I keep expecting something to resurface there, something to keep me from moving.

When I turned out the lights that night, the sun hadn't gone down yet. Sarah my Facebook roommate was out in the kitchen frying pre-packaged hash browns on our stove that has to be lit with a match and I could smell her cooking spray heating in the pan. I put the inside of my elbow over my eyes and imagined I spent a decade working at a kitchen store, and I knew every kind of cooking knife in the world, and I had dedicated myself to unlearning the idea of a structured, moral universe where my soul mattered because other people had used this concept to terrorize me in my childhood, and I really loved a dying ferret, and I also loved a guy who had a lot of problems with my personality but was in too deep now to leave me. I imagined being in a submarine and imagining that the submarine was underwater.

Yes, I thought, feeling it more intensely than I thought I would, starting to cry without understanding it, *We have somewhere to go.*

Picked up all the dry and perfect squash. We walked up and down the rows piling them, then Boss brought the tractor down the middle of the field with enormous plastic bins on the front loader forks. We filled them in a fire line, two people throwing to two people counting aloud so Boss could make tally marks on his clipboard from where he sat on the tractor. Got a couple thousand squash and kept our sweatshirts on until lunch.

Boss offered me winter work to replace Kristy, three days a week harvesting greens and weeding in the hoop houses for the CSA. I didn't know she decided to leave and I don't think I'll take it. My world here has changed so much I'd be starting over even if I stayed, and I am ready to move. Taking this job might have been the first truly brave thing I ever did in my life and I feel brave enough now for whatever is next. Still, I feel guilty and scared to say no.

On the drive home I asked Kristy why she stayed so long. She said she worked on nonprofit farms before, which are much less pressure and don't drive you as hard because they have no real bottom line, and she liked this better because it really mattered. Then she said she is leaving because it's clear this farm specifically is never going to give anything back to her. That's what happens when you try to make something your own that nobody ever told you could be yours, probably, but she must know that.

We all know that in a single digit number of weeks, we are leaving, which makes it hard to care much for the rest of our stay. That's what I think, anyhow.

Pena is back at college and only comes into work twice a week. He talked so little, but I really notice when he is not here. Our team mindset has almost disintegrated; we don't eat lunch together anymore or make up new running jokes.

Perhaps we are coming apart without him to be our audience, without the knowledge that someone is watching us, or maybe it's just something that happens.

We spent the morning clipping the dry tops off of the onions in the greenhouse and piling them into black crates bound for the walk-in coolers. The snips were dull and sticky. It took a long time to arrange ourselves in an efficient workflow. Kristy made a lot of angry faces before losing her temper, and Gwynn yelled back that she was sick of being micromanaged, and I clenched my teeth so hard I feared they'd crack.

I don't know how you survive it, Pena said to me in his little voice while we walked to the barn for lunch, shaking his tiny head, Working here all week still. I just don't know how you do it.

At his slowest he works better than I ever will, and at his worst he contains himself better than I ever could. The idea that he doesn't even enjoy it just will not fit in my mind. What pushes him on? I felt special to be doing something that impressed him and I wished I didn't. Just because I'm two years older and one foot taller, I think I should have it all figured out.

I've got this pet theory that you can tell most of what you need to know about a person by how they relate to difficulty—whether it is a punishment to escape, a lesson to learn, something to bear, or once in a long while, a gift. I don't get to test this theory out very often because most environments I've been in focused on minimizing personal pain.

I figured Pena had somehow just transcended all this,

but it's as hard on him as it is on me.

While pitchforking carrots with mud-cold hands in field 4B that afternoon, I tried asking God to carry me through it again and felt my heart physically sputter, backfiring like the cars that drive by my rented window in the dark.

Boss mentioned casually as we washed up at the end of the day that he can't remember the last time he fed the chickens, which live in a coop behind his house where we never see them. Just can't deal with it, he said, and speculated that several had likely starved to death, maybe even tried to cannibalize each other, if any remained alive.

He said this while eating a peanut butter sandwich and smiling, but not in any sick way, just like it was truly incidental to him.

Turned down the winter work today. For some reason I phrased it like a real asshole: That won't work for me, is what I said inside the barn at the end of the day.

Oh, okay, no worries, Boss replied in this small voice, hosing off bundles of beets, wearing his big green rubber apron. What are you going to do?

I told him I was really making plans to move, and he said Oh, cool. He honestly looked sad. Maybe he was thinking of the time spent training me, and how much more efficient I could have been next season if I wasn't doing everything for the first time.

I have no idea what will happen and I haven't made any plans. I've just got to do it, got to do it, the way I had to do this. Walking away across the concrete expanse of the wash room, I tried to keep Gwynn's voice in my mind about how nobody owes anybody anything, or whatever.

Sitting next to Kristy in her cold car that smelled like cigarettes, I had a feeling like I did when I first got hired here, that something I couldn't have hoped for was becoming possible, in spite of all my shortcomings, and it was more than I could personally contain.

It rains almost every day now. We slip everywhere we walk. The tractor leaves deep ruts that will linger for years in the muddy pathways, and twelve-foot-wide puddles have opened up in the driveway.

Yesterday we harvested two thousand pounds of cabbage to clear the beds out. The cut stems poke out from a thick layer of rotting or worm-eaten leaves peeled away and dropped to return into the soil. When the cold rain falls, you lose feeling in your hands almost immediately. Your hair is soaked and you can't see and you won't be warm for another eight hours, but you do it anyway.

No more planting or weeding except for the salad greens in the hoop houses, which will grow through winter. Of everything we do, I like harvesting the best. Sometimes when I tell my mother I don't know whether I'm doing the right things or not, she says, Look at the fruits. Nothing's gotten easier for me, but I think I've gotten a little better.

We pulled beets in the rain all day today and yesterday, shuffling down the beds with our legs on either side and yanking the three rows up by their greens in handfuls of six or seven. Then we cut the tops with harvest knives and piled them in dirty white five-gallon buckets. When we harvest fresh for market, we leave the greens on and rubber-band them, but these ones will be bagged to stay in the cooler all winter. They last longer when they're bald.

Pena arrived in the spring with his own little leather sheath for the harvest knife that he wore on his belt, but now he uses the dull ones that hang from their serrated blades on a magnet strip in the wash barn like the rest of us. He lost his, a birthday present, in a carrot bed in July.

The celery-like pink stalks come up from the top of the beet and widen out into palm-sized leaves. They stained our fingers pink where we cut them into short clumps at the top. Many of the greens were slick and rotting and spotted with black blight circles; together with the rain and mud, none of us could keep a grasp on anything, dropping the beets and our knives and our cell phones.

Gwynn sat in the muck between beds while she

worked, sliding around inefficiently on her hands and knees like a baby. Pena and I made a lot of eye contact because we could tell Kristy was angry about this. He had brought us donuts in the morning, said he woke up at four forty-five for them. For his own lunch he ate a palm-sized amount of plain ground beef from a plastic container. He told me once that black pepper gives him crippling heartburn.

Hauled the beets up to the barn, washed them, packed them into fifty-pound plastic bags to live in the cooler, struggled to steer the pallet jack in there. As always, I failed to gather fast enough or to fill my buckets as fast as Kristy, which I think is why she put me on hauling duty. The buckets are cracked and broken especially around the handles and cannot ever be stacked on each other, because then they will never come apart again, so I carried them all from the bed to the golf cart on my hip and was coated with cold mud.

In the barn, I emptied the beets into the barrel washer and skidded the golf cart back down the grass paths to where everyone else was huddled. You don't have to worry about bruising beets like some other vegetables, can pour them right onto the wood from any old height. Boss ran the washer, standing with the hose in one hand and the other on his hip, looking out over the fields like a king.

Kristy and I snapped at each other and then joked about getting Boss' accident insurance to cover bionic arm replacements, which we could program so as to be better farmers. We don't get health insurance so that's really our only hope.

We have also started to talk about next season. None of us are returning here, but somehow it is never a question that we will keep farming—just somewhere else. Kristy might go to California, Gwynn to a farm with a reasonable commute, Pena in his parents' backyard, me back where I came from.

I think occasionally about doing something else, these sorts of formless ideas about helping other people somehow beyond growing boutique vegetables for the wealthy, but if I say it out loud, no one seems to hear me, no one responds.

All week we've been saying, As ye sow, so shall ye reap!, which works especially well when we harvest beets that are hollow from too much water or broccoli heads deformed and black from disease.

Phantom tremors in my ring finger.

Can't understand my own unwillingness to drink water.

Forgot my winter hat outside the barn and mice chewed the top of it right off overnight.

Now that most everything is out of the fields, we've started to un-staple and roll up the plastic landscape fabric. The sheets are three feet wide and half an acre long, stuck down on either side of each row. When we start in the morning the fabric is frozen stiff with dew and our hands get hard to use. My feet go numb inside my boots from the cold earth. Instead of discussing church, Gwynn wants to talk about labor relations.

Sunrises are bleached and we've pushed our starting time back to eight.

It stayed warm almost all September after that first cold snap and now, suddenly, the winter—no fall to speak of. We work silently more than we talk now, but when I leave, I feel just as embarrassed as always. Though the heat and hysteria of peak summer overloaded me in seemingly every way, I almost miss it now.

It was beautiful out this afternoon, sunny-cold, and I've been feeling bad about how every day I come home from work and go right to bed, so I took the bus to the park on the west side where Red and I used to walk around when he lived here.

Hiked into the woods and up the hill but only felt a tight paranoia spiraling in around my shoulders. I experimented with being glum but there's just a little nothing-space where the feelings were, unless of course I think about them for too long. I want to be someone who can control what happens after that but I often find I just have to try again the next day. Without anyone here to tell me what species they are, all the plants look the same.

I can come so close to forgetting everything I ever did or was before—on larger scales, like remembering Red and Anne and Nate and the place before this one and the place before that, and on smaller ones, like coming out here tonight when in the morning I was on the farm. I know how to do a few more things and I'm a little older now.

Sat by the pond to write and watched an old man Frisbee whole slices of white bread to the ducks, standing under the sign that reads DO NOT FEED DUCKS.

Packaged a lot of salad, tried to correct my posture, washed a lot of harvest bins. Yeah yeah yeah.

I only feel like myself anymore when I walk to the store on a Monday and buy deli-sliced Cajun turkey for $6.99 per pound, when I have one day out of the week that I can direct. That's more than half an hour of my labor.

It's so strange and new to be loose in the world during the day, even just for a few minutes like this. I almost want to ask if I'm allowed here. I'm not sure what kind of person I will emerge as when the work is done. Soon I'll be able to do this all the time and maybe after a little while I won't even notice anymore.

Found a tree frog in the wash barn while we scrubbed salad harvest bins today. Even now, in October! We stopped working to gather around and marvel at it all scrunched up on one of the yellow crates we use for transport to market. It was smaller than my thumb and so bright, almost minty-colored. It wore a calm, sincere smile.

Gwynn didn't try to pick it up this time. I've really never felt such a small thing mean so much to everybody around me in the exact same way. Maybe we were all tired or maybe we had been feeling like nothing new was ever going to happen.

Kristy talked about it all day, and we were so unused to seeing her happy that we yelled it back and forth with her while we harvested deformed rutabagas in another cold rain—Tree frog on the harvest bin! Frog in a barn!

I saw three people carrying swords at market today: one in a holster at the waist, another across the chest, the third stuffed inside a backpack with the handle and half the hilt banging against the back of the man's head from the unevenness of his gait.

Three separate people at three separate times.

Ryan's stall was empty, because his mother is taking an extended vacation to Florida and hasn't made any new acorn people. He texted me a photo of a muddy campsite up north somewhere. I asked him what it was like and he didn't respond; I tried hard not to feel that I'm the same wretched person as before, saying the wrong thing.

In the morning, sitting on the stoop in the dark waiting for Boss to pick me up, a man walked by in jangling spurs, followed shortly by another wrapped head to toe in Christmas lights.

Well, why not?

Tore up the tomato hoop house yesterday and today. We unclipped all the plants from their twines, cut them at the bases, hauled the bodies out, unstapled and shook apart and rolled the landscape fabric, pulled up all the roots, cleaned out the wrinkled fallen fruits.

Now that it is gone, I miss it, I miss that place, that funny thing, that hot house where I worked for so long harvesting something I don't even like to eat.

Spinach goes in later.

We don't laugh much while we work now. Kristy told me there are two or three months of every year when farmers feel toward their life: "Fuck this."

I would hate to live that way, but already I can tell it will be difficult to stay away from this, from the pressure and the cycles that are always so clear and how I always know what the air feels like and that things can be difficult and real, and maybe I will never be able to again. Since I already admitted I came here because I was afraid, I feel brave enough to speculate that even if I do this again, it will be because I chose to, not because it was all I could believe in, or because I thought I had choices but didn't really.

We're starting work close to eight-thirty now because the sunrise has moved back so far, which nobody likes because it means we get home so late, when the day is basically over. I never had the energy to do much anyway, but it was nice to know of the possibility. Gwynn and her boyfriend are thinking about adopting a greyhound. The leaves should be turning, but it's been so warm this fall that most trees are green and then barren, with no color in between. The leaves skitter across the dirt roads just the same, houses and yards emerging from behind them.

Read this weekend that progress can never be made by viewing suffering as a problem to be solved. We live; we suffer. Nothing ever goes away, or our needs for things never do, anyhow.

Harvested rows fourteen through seventeen of the potatoes today, with six left to go. All week, just potatoes. We were crawling, scrabbling through the dirt, sifting potatoes in our hands and piling them in black plastic crates, and my knees made their same old cap gun pop when I bent to lift them on the back of the golf cart. Yer dead!

We weigh the crates with a scale on the back of the golf cart, label them with the variety and stack them in the cooler. We don't wash them first. Leaving the dirt on is a natural preservative, Boss said, like the invisible layer on fresh chicken eggs.

After work, Tiny and I went to a guitar concert at a new place downtown with a huge octopus painted on the floor, its tentacles touching every wall. Other than her and Shane, I don't want to see anyone anymore, am ready to give it all a rest. She picked me up from my apartment in his sedan and I felt like hiding the dirt cracked into my fingers when we paid for our tickets.

Behind the card table where the ticket sellers sat was a shaky cardboard confessional with puppet show curtains instructing you to write your sins on its walls in scented marker. Other people before us had scrawled out jokes. I LOVE TOO HARD, ICE CREAM FOR DINNER, HIT FROM THE BACK. We didn't write anything. Of all the people I've known, Tiny is the only one who will act differently around me because of what I tell her about myself, even apologizes for using the Lord's name in vain, which makes me feel kind of embarrassed because I didn't ask her to and don't really care about that kind of thing to the degree I probably should, but I appreciate it so much.

Left the show in the middle to drink tap water, from my cupped hands in the bathroom because the fountains had masking tape over them. When I returned, the artist was explaining that the tuning of her guitar was believed by the Norwegians to invite the devil into the room, and the audience laughed.

It makes me nervous that so few people seem to take good and evil seriously. Then again, I can't talk about either thing with Gwynn, who does care, without feeling like it will kill us both or crush something very important and fragile that I'm holding in my hand. In one sense, nothing that happens on earth really matters, but at the same time how we move through it is our only real way of demonstrating what we understand about everything else above it.

Walking back to the car in the cold, circling behind the squat Dutch church where we'd parked, I remembered my high school boyfriend saying I protect myself too much by keeping my thoughts and feelings so contained. *But I'm all I have*, I had thought then, and remembering it, I realized it isn't really true anymore.

Tiny pointed out as she started the engine that the church in front of us had such a long mansard roof that it almost reached the ground, just a few inches of wall visible above the parking lot. I thought it was funny and she didn't really, but that was fine. We had a good time and then I went home and walked up the driveway and turned on the lights and there I was, moving around in the world, for some reason.

It's too cold in the mornings now to enjoy waiting outside to get picked up, but I sit on the steps anyways to give myself a few minutes of life when nothing happens. There are always cars driving down the quiet side street, even at this hour.

I think sometimes I'll die and only leave behind things I created in this world, not take anything rotten out of it with me, spat from my mouth to the side of a purgatorial road. Cut an eye from a potato, plant a new one in the spring. Say good morning to Kristy, say nothing afterwards, try to listen for what to do.

We planted next year's garlic today: covered the field with compost first, marked the holes, stuck the cloves in and buried them with straw. It's cheaper to buy cloves from someone else and plant them than use the stuff we grew last season. Before all that, we shoveled compost out of the tractor bucket and across the field while Boss filled it from the giant heap out past the greenhouse. Last time we flung compost was in late spring, preparing the onion fields. Hurts less to do it now although I've got less energy.

While we pushed the cloves down into the cold thin soil and covered them, Kristy and Gwynn and I talked about what we ate for dinner last night and what we would eat for dinner tonight. When Kristy went to the barn for water I asked Gwynn if she'd changed her mind about heaven and she said she hadn't decided. Boss was chopping wood up by his house and we could hear the ax falls ringing. It was cold and close to snowing. The sky looked like sundown all day.

Kristy drove us home fast and crazy like she couldn't wait for the ride to be over. The guy who burns leaves in his yard every single day was at it again. Although I'm still trying to give up my control and not respond so much to what other people do, I can't help thinking about how this season would have gone differently if I were a better person. The leaf guy is pretty much the only subject Kristy and I can comfortably speak about now; I always feel relieved when we're near his house and one of us is about to make a joke. We never see him, though—only the smoking pile he's left out front. He could be anyone.

Our last week went by slower than death. When I get home every night, I go online to look at jobs I am not qualified for and apartments I cannot afford, and I believe it will work. I could totally be a resident of Massachusetts. Thursday it was raining ice, and Boss said we could stay home if we wanted to, but only if the whole crew agreed. Kristy texted me separately the words *Say no.*

I stayed home and vacuumed the rugs and cleaned my baseboards and could have chewed through my bottom lip, probably, from all the energy of my life about to change. Red asked to call me, and I forgot to write back. It feels like the foundation just dropped out from everything. Still, I'm making plans for the soup I'll cook on Saturday and the movie I'll watch with Shane and Tiny on Monday and wondering if I should risk going to confession over the weekend, as if nothing like this has ever consumed me.

We met in the wash barn today to review the season. Two sheets of butcher paper had been taped to the harvest whiteboard titled WORKED and NEEDS WORK. I looked forward to this all season, but sitting at the bin-scrubbing table and smelling the hydrogen peroxide hanging around it, I could barely remember anything or what I thought about it. Boss had never asked for our input before. He stood on the other side of the table looking pained and solitary, like a sea-stunted pine tree growing from a cliff.

We ate chunky, flavorless hummus from paper plates and scrutinized row cover storage and irrigation strategies and harvest workflow. Boss listened to Kristy and Pena, told Gwynn and I there were things we did not understand yet, kept driving the marker cap into his palm. Without movement to make you pay attention to the minutes, seven hours pass like nothing.

Then we were gathered in the driveway hugging, maybe from a sense of duty rather than any real desire, but duty makes the world go round after all. Gwynn asked me to be her pen pal, and Pena said I could come play badminton next summer if I was still here, and I wanted to cry about something ending but Kristy was already in her car with the engine running.

Everything goes on without us; somebody just needs to fill the space. Real work appears to depend on and reflect something other than the quality of your character or the development of your mind, an expendability that can put you in your place (which is having no place). But really it does reflect us, how careful or how skilled or how strong we can wait to become.

I feel closer to the world than before—the one I used to ask God to let me be part of, the foundation of it all, everything that lived out here while the rest of us sat in classrooms and offices. I hoped this year would make me harder to hurt. Instead it made me listen.

Kristy braked hard at the first stoplight on the edge of the city, twisting her palms and fingers around the rubber wrapping of the steering wheel while we waited for green. The sunlight was already narrowing over the empty cornfields. Pretty soon I'll bend without noticing it, and the skin on my hands will be clean. I'll find out if someone else really was preparing to emerge from within me all along, and that will be just as natural as every other thing that happens.

Flurries by the windshield and news on the radio.

Acknowledgements

I'm thankful to my parents, my teachers, Johnathan, Molly and strangers on the internet for their belief in and support of my writing. My eternal thanks to Lena Crown for choosing to publish this book, working so carefully and thoughtfully with me through the editing process and encouraging me to be vulnerable; thanks to Michael Wheaton for his time and dedication getting it over the finish line, and for bringing Autofocus Books into being. The ideas and experiences in this story were only possible for me to share because many, many people have dedicated their efforts to trying to live differently. I appreciate all of them.

About the Author

E.N. Couturier is an award-winning journalist and recreational farmer. *Organic Matter* is her first book. Her work has appeared in numerous Maine news outlets, on local radio and in publications including *New World Writing, Peripheries, Eclectica Magazine, FRiGG,* and *jmww,* and has been nominated for Best of the Net and the Pushcart Prize. She never did go to graduate school.

— also from Autofocus Books —

Duplex — Mike Nagel

XO — Sara Rauch

Until It Feels Right — Emily Costa

Cleave — Holly Pelesky

Nextdoor in Colonialtown — Ryan Rivas

Too Much Tongue — Adrienne Marie Barrios & Leigh Chadwick

Picture Window — Danny Caine

the nature machine! — Tyler Gillespie

A Kind of In-Between — Aaron Burch

How to Write a Novel: An Anthology of 20 Craft Essays About Writing, None of Which Ever Mention Writing — ed. Aaron Burch

Hiraeth — Mistie R. Watkins

That Spell — Tate N. Oquendo

My Modest Blindness — Russell Brakefield

A Calendar Is A Snakeskin — Kristine Langley Mahler

Culdesac — Mike Nagel

Razed by TV Sets — Jason McCall

In the Away Time — Kristen E. Nelson

The Body Is A Temporary Gathering Place — Andrew Bertaina

Daughterhood — Emily Adrian

A Healthy Interest in the Lives of Others — Teresa Carmody

Yes I Am Human I Know You Were Wondering — Erin Dorney

Leave: A Postpartum Account — Shayne Terry

Out There In the Dark — Katharine Coldiron

If I Can Be Honest: Selected Prose from the Four Years of Autofocus Lit (2020-2024)— ed. Michael Wheaton

www.ingramcontent.com/pod-product-compliance
Lightning Source LLC
LaVergne TN
LVHW050959080826
845145LV00009B/2354

* 9 7 8 1 9 5 7 3 9 2 3 8 7 *